The Other Side of the Law

Paul Reed

with Crystal Crawford

Disclaimer:

This work depicts actual events in the life of the author, told as truthfully as recollection permits. While all persons within are actual individuals, some names and identifying characteristics have been changed to respect their privacy.

To those of you who signed the waivers allowing me to use your full names in this book—thank you. Coming up with fake names for everyone would've been a challenge, plus it's a lot more fun to see your actual names reflected on these pages. Thanks for your support of this book, and for being a part of my life. The stories in this book wouldn't exist without you.

Note:

I do know grammar—but this book is written like I'm telling you the story, not like a paper I would turn in to the 2nd District Court of Appeals. Some stylistic choices have been made to preserve the informal tone of the book, and to keep it authentic to how I would've told it if you were sitting across the table from me, in person.

Table of Contents

Introduction

The general public has an opinion about lawyers. Without quoting words I've promised my co-author not to use in this book, it boils down to this: They are not one of *us*. They come from money. They're dishonest, and don't really care about their clients—like the old joke firm Dewey, Cheatem and Howe. Their mom and dad paid for their school. They come from privilege and advantage. At worst, they're out for themselves, and at best, they're out of touch, far removed from the down-to-earth lives of "the rest of us." They were born with a silver spoon.

I was not.

This book will show you another side of the law. It won't always be pretty, but it will be real. It will be honest. It will tell how I got from A to Z—from the redneck orange groves of Brandon, FL to owning and running one of the top-performing law firms in the Tampa Bay area. It will tell parts of law school and law life you might not believe if I didn't have pictures. (I do.) It will show you my heart behind what I do, and that there really are lawyers who care about their clients.

These stories probably won't be what you expect. But they are true stories. They are *my* stories.

They are the other side of the law.

–Paul

Part I

Orange Groves and Trailer Parks

Chapter 1

◆─○───────────○─◆

Small Town Brandon
Back in the Day

The House on Larson Avenue

Like all people, my memories of my earliest years are vague at best. I was born on July 22, 1964. I had one brother two years older than me (Jody), and a younger brother by about eighteen months (Keith). I had a mom, of course. And for a time, I had a dad.

We lived in a trailer park, and at some point before I can remember, we moved into the house at 203 Larson Avenue, only two miles from where our Reed & Reed office is today. The house on Larson was a concrete block home, and small by many of today's standards. It was just under 1200 square feet, with three bedrooms about ten by ten feet each, a living room, a small kitchen, two bathrooms, and no air conditioning. The inside of the house was decorated simply, with the fashion of the day: beige walls, gold curtains, table lamps with beige lampshades, and furniture in shades of gold, orange, or brown. We had a plush armchair covered in velvety, dark orange fabric, and dark wood furniture accented with deep green potted plants and a bright green, sculpted ashtray. A miniature, grandfather-style clock hung on the wall by the front door.

Our house did not have many of the features modern day homes have. Microwave oven? Never heard of that growing up. Cable TV? What was that? There were no locks on the door... that, I miss. We didn't have a dishwasher at first, but when we got one, we were very excited! It was great, but it wasn't like dishwashers today. For one thing, it hooked up to the sink to turn on. We'd have to take out all the cords and hook it up before we could use it. Also, it was huge. It wouldn't fit inside a cabinet, so it just sat in the corner of the kitchen against the door, and we moved it around as needed. If we needed to cook, we moved it into the next room where the dining table was. When we wanted to wash dishes, we moved it back into the kitchen. So the dishwasher got run at night when everybody went to bed, and other than that, we just worked around it or moved it. We all loved that dishwasher!

The Living Room on Larson Avenue
I always wanted a grandfather clock but could not remember why until writing this book and finding this picture.

We had a little television in the living room, a big box-style contraption with a small, nineteen-inch screen set inside it. There was no cable TV—it didn't exist yet, at least not at our house. So we had a huge, thirty-foot antenna outside the house. We only got about four channels: 8, 10, 13, 44... and maybe PBS. Channels 10 and 44 were brutal to tune in. Someone would have to go outside and turn the giant antenna by hand to get those channels to show up. The others would be inside, yelling, "Hey, go back! Go back the other way! Stop, stop, that's good!" Once it was tuned in, the person moving the antenna would go back inside to watch TV with everyone else. If we decided we wanted to change the channel again, someone would have to go back outside to turn the antenna. It really sucked when it was raining, because there was nothing to do *but* watch TV, so someone would have to go outside in the rain. Eventually, we got a little dial on the TV that would turn the outside antenna for us, and we were like, "Woohoo! We're filthy rich!"

The yard out front was not very large, and was just grass—no fancy landscaping or shrubbery. Behind the house was a big open field, and across the street from the front of the house, there was a four- to five-acre field with a pond. Nowadays, that acreage is overgrown, fenced off with a house next to it, and the pond is a dried-up drainage ditch. But back then, it was *our* pond, and we played in it all the time. We didn't own it, but that was a technicality. To us and to our friends in the neighborhood, it was ours.

At some point later on, we got a pool put in the backyard—a vinyl fiberglass one, not a fancy concrete one, but we had a pool! We were living large.

Larson Avenue began at Parsons Avenue (a high-traffic road) and ended at Horace Mann Junior High. There were five houses between our house and Parsons, and five houses in the other direction between our house and Horace Mann. My friends and I used Horace Mann as our playground. You wouldn't be able to do this today—there's a fence out front, and if a big gang of kids came and raced through the property like we did, someone would probably call the cops—but back then, Horace Mann was wide open. It had monkey bars, swings, a basketball court, a football field with actual field goals, and open hallways perfect for riding bikes. It even had a teeter totter.

The main road behind Horace Mann—Kingsway Road—is a busy strip of businesses and shops, these days, with neighborhoods and houses tucked down side streets. But back then, Kingsway was mostly orange groves, with the exception of the "rich" neighborhood. (They even had their own community swimming pool.)

We had a great group of guys in our neighborhood. Wally, Larry, Gary, and Fred were older, but we all played together. Then there were Hal, Lee, Roy, Wayne, Donald, Chris, and too many others to name, all within biking or walking distance of Horace Mann.

Wally and Larry's family had some money; they owned Brandon Supply store, the only hardware store in Brandon at the time.

Today, that two-acre lot on the north corner of Larson is a big church, but back then, it was where Wally and Larry lived. Wally was probably two years older than Jody, and Larry was a year older than Wally, but the age difference didn't matter for playing sports together—we were all good; Wally played on the high school team, and Jody eventually went to the big leagues. As kids, that's nearly all we did, from the time the sun rose until it set, except for when we were at school. On Saturdays, we would get up as quietly as we could and try to get out of the house, because if Mom was up first, she'd put us to work. (We had removed the screen on the window by the front door so that our dog, Zeke, could come in and out when he wanted to... so instead of opening the door, we climbed out the window.)

Even on school days, we'd come home and play. Wally and Larry had a barn, and a corral with horses, a pony, and a pig named Grunt. Their property was where we'd play baseball. Home plate was their big hickory nut tree facing Parsons, and the barn was the edge of the outfield. We'd play two on two, Wally and me versus Larry and Jody, or whatever. Just a pitcher and outfielder. There was a tree right in the middle of the property, in the outfield. If we hit the ball to the right side of the tree, we were out. If anyone ever wonders why Jody got to the big leagues and

---

Zeke

We were never without a dog during my childhood. We had lots of dogs over the years, and they just roamed the house, the yard, and the neighborhood. There was no fence or leash.

Zeke, the dog we had when I was young, was a golden retriever. When we went to play, he would just follow us—to Horace Mann, to the pond, or wherever.

Zeke would also leave for two to three days at a time. We wouldn't see him, then he'd come back exhausted.

One time, a neighbor brought a container full of puppies, said, "These are yours," then dropped them off and left. They were Zeke's puppies. (Back then, people didn't neuter their pets; it just wasn't a thing, yet. I guess that's why Bob Barker made such a big deal about it on *The Price is Right*.)

I was heading that way myself, this is why—we got really good at aiming our hits. The telephone pole was on the third base side of our baseball field, the tree was dead center field, and we had to hit it in between, or we were out. If we hit it onto the barn, that was a home run... but the outfielder could catch it as it rolled off the roof of the barn. So we'd run up to the barn, jump, catch the ball—*You're out!*

Gary lived across from Wally and Larry, three houses down from us. Gary was about four or five years older than me, and his parents were divorced, so it was just Gary, his mom (Ms. Linda), and his sister Mary Linda. She was about my age, and by default, a tomboy. But by and large, the neighborhood was a gang of guys.

We would play baseball at Wally and Larry's, basketball in our driveway (we had a hoop above our garage nailed right into the roof!), football at Horace Mann, and orange wars in the groves. If you've never heard of orange wars, it was a game where we would break into two teams. One team would go to one side of the area we'd chosen, the other team would go to the other side, and then we'd converge and start blasting each other with oranges.

We also dug a tunnel fort in the field behind us, rode bikes, played in the pond, went skateboarding, camped out, and went to Lithia Springs. Everything we played, we played hard, we played to win, and we played until somebody usually got hurt. Other than injuries, the only thing that stopped us from playing was Mom calling us home for dinner. We didn't sit around the house, period. We played from sun up until the sun set.

It was one heck of a neighborhood.

Mom, Jody, Keith, and Me

My mom was young and attractive when we were kids—she'd had all three of us boys by the time she was twenty-two. In my memories and in pictures from back then, she's slim, well-dressed, and classy, with tasteful makeup and carefully styled hair, just flat out beautiful. She's still like that today, actually. Mom's always been a looker. Even in her seventies, she still gets random compliments when she goes out.

Jim Reed was my "dad." He was five-foot-eleven with black hair and brown eyes, a good looking man. He was on the last H.B. Plant High School State Championship basketball team. Although he got a basketball scholarship to college, he joined the Marines instead. Honestly, I don't really have much to say about my dad, because he left when I was about four years old, and was never around after that. One afternoon, while working at the Bank of America building as an attorney in downtown Tampa, I ran into him. He was not facing in my direction, so I didn't know how to get his attention. I'd never called him *Dad* after he left, and I didn't feel comfortable calling him *Jim*

Mom, back then.

because growing up, you did not call adults by their first names. So I finagled myself into a position where he could see me, and I just said, "Hey." Talk about awkward— that's an understatement.

I have two distinct memories of Dad/Jim from the years before he left. In one, Jim, Grandpa Reed, and our neighbor, Mr. Glenn, were installing an air conditioner in our home, one of those old wall units. They placed it in the garage, where it could shoot down the hall.

Mom, Jim, Me, Keith, and Jody

PAUL REED

That air conditioner was a steadier presence in my life than my dad was.

The only other thing I really remember about him was the day he left. To this day, in my mind I think we were under a tornado watch or a hurricane was coming, but in reality, it could've been just a typical, violent summer storm with lightning. To me, that day was like the end of the earth. He and my mom got into a fight, and he just... left. I remember crying, begging him to stay. He didn't.

And that was it; he was gone.

Later, I had two step dads at different points in my life—John Morrell, for about five years (ages ten to fifteen), and Stinger (from age twenty until he passed away a few years ago). They were both good guys, and the closest things to a dad I ever had. In the early years, though, it was just Mom, Jody, Keith, and me, in the house on Larson Avenue.

Me, Keith, and Jody during one of our football seasons.

When Jim left, Mom was only about twenty-five years old. She'd had Jody when she was eighteen, me at twenty, and Keith at twenty-two. There was a daughter too, between Jody and me, who died a few days after birth. (So we would've had a sister. Wow, wouldn't that have been cool!) We never talked about that, ever, other than the conversation where we found out about her.

Raising three Reed boys was a total handful for Mom. She was young, and we were hellions. But she made us breakfast, went to all our games, and took us places—there was 100 percent love. We never doubted that at all. There's not a woman who ever loved her children more than Mom.

Mom was a nurse. She worked all the time. There was no sil-

Mom with Keith, Me, and Jody

ver spoon at 203 Larson Avenue. If there happened to be some dinner left over after we all got servings, whoever ate fastest got seconds. To this day, if you watch Jody or me eat, we still scarf down our food. We weren't rich, but we also weren't poor. Life was good.

Mom made sure we took our studies seriously, and she made sure we were involved in every sport Brandon had to offer. During football season we played football, in basketball season we'd play basketball with the county league, and in baseball season we played at North Brandon Little League (NBLL), which was behind Yates Elementary at that time. At one point, I was even in a competitive bowling league.

We would spend most nights on that Little League field: Mom was the NBLL designated score-keeper. We were there almost every night... except on Wednesday night or Sundays, of course, because those nights, we were at church. We attended Sunday school and church weekly. We also went to a lot of movies with Mom, back then, and big

Me, Jody, and Keith during one of our baseball seasons

nights out were trips to the Waffle House or Whataburger, where we would eat in the car (kind of like Sonic today). I think there are still some Whataburgers around, though not in Brandon anymore. During the summer time, we were always at one body of water or another, whether it be the beach, Lake Ellen, or Lithia Springs.

My brother Jody and I were together twenty-four seven. We played every sport together, rode bikes together, more or less did *everything* together. I was on the shy side, but Jody was a ladies' man. Our younger brother, Keith, was more of a fighter. He didn't take crap from anyone. For whatever reason, Jody and I did not hang out as much with Keith. Keith had his own friends, and just tended to do his own thing with the kids his age. Jody was mom's favorite. He could do whatever he wanted. But Mom really had her

Come Hell or High Water

I was in a bowling league for a while as a kid, and I was pretty good. So during the champion game, I was bowling against a girl, and we were neck and neck. I slipped, fell, and the bowling ball landed on my right hand and broke my finger. And I was right-handed.

God bless Mom—knowing my competitive spirit and can't lose attitude, she allowed me to keep playing. My hand swelled up so much, I couldn't even get my fingers in the holes. I had to bowl by rolling the ball with two hands, but I wasn't about to lose to a girl. I was going to finish that game, come hell or high water.

I was crying, trying to bowl, bending over, bowling with my left hand—finally, Mom made me leave, and I lost by default.

I remember crying all the way to the hospital, not because my hand was in pain, but because I couldn't finish the game.

hands full with all three of us. Jody was a pretty boy, I was super smart and stubborn, and Keith was such a little terror, everyone just left him alone; he was kinda scary. There's a picture I'll include here, from when we were about nine, ten, or eleven—Jody's got this flowing, long blonde hair. Keith and I have bowl cuts Mom just gave us at home, but not Jody; he went to the beauty salon to get his hair cut. Mom won't admit it, Jody won't admit it... but when Keith was still here, he'd back me up: Jody was the favorite. Period.

The Margison Clan

As I said earlier, being a single mom of three boys, Mom worked a lot. To say overtime pay was important would not do that statement justice. There was a neighborhood family, the Margisons, who had ten kids: seven boys and three girls. They were at our house so often, it seemed like they lived with us. In fact, one of them, Ricky, actually did live with us at one point. Having someone there to help watch us

Jody (top left), with Keith (middle), and me (top right). Keith and I are modeling our bowl cuts.

allowed Mom to juggle being a single parent, working, and trying to have some semblance of a life of her own. Ricky wasn't strict with us—we wouldn't have listened to him if he had been. We enjoyed him living with us. Ricky moved in and stayed until graduating from high school and joining the army. About that time, we were old enough to stay by ourselves whenever Mom wasn't home.

I'm still close with all the Margisons. The Margisons were, and still are, family. As of this writing, I have represented both Joanne, Roy, and Ricky for motor vehicle crashes, plus Wayne for an assault and battery at an Orlando drinking establishment, and have gotten money for all of them.

One of the eight Margisons, Roy, was my age. We were friends at birth and remain friends to this day. We still grab a beer on occasion.

Like I said, the Margisons weren't really authority figures when they were at our house, but we also didn't give them much trouble. We went to school, played, then came home, and one of them would have dinner ready for us. We'd eat, do homework, watch TV, maybe play a game or whatever, and go to bed.

Being boys, we made up crazy games to play. We had one game where somebody would stand at the end of the hallway with a BB gun. Then we'd put pillows and blankets in front of the closet door at the end of the hallway, and the other kids would run back and forth across the hallway between the bedrooms, being shot at by the person with the BB gun until someone got hit. When you got hit, your prize was you got to be the shooter next. We had to aim from the waist down, so there were no major injuries, but being hit stung bad. That was one game we'd play while Mom was at work, and Ricky would even play it with us.

Oranges

Growing up, our snacks were oranges picked fresh from the nearby groves. Mom, God bless her, provided the main meals—but for snacks we'd go through the orange grove with a paper bag from Publix, and fill it up with oranges. We had a little old-school juice squeezer that spun around, so we made our own orange juice, and oranges were our snack. For lunches, we had peanut butter and jelly or a bologna sandwich, with oranges and maybe some chips —so we ate a lot of oranges. I still love oranges.

We had another game called "Lights Out." Jody, Ricky, Roy, Keith, and I would all play it together. We'd close all the curtains so the house was pitch black. One person would be "It" and would go out to the garage where the electric box was while everyone else hid. The "It" person would turn off the electricity, then come back in and try to find everyone. Once he found someone, he'd have to hold on to the person while screaming, "Lights! Lights!" until someone else made their way to the garage to flip the breaker. Whoever was "It" had to still be holding onto the person he'd found when the lights came back on. Sometimes, you'd be getting the heck beat out of you holding on, screaming, "Lights! Lights!" We'd play that for *hours*. Here's the problem with the Lights Out game: Mom got bored easily. What do I mean by that statement? Well, she would move the furniture on a regular basis. One time, I was running from somebody, and I thought I was gonna dive-bomb onto the bed. Well, Mom had moved the bed, so I hit the oak dresser—*bam.* Unconscious. Someone heard the thump, turned on the lights... and it was "Lights Out" for me. That's when the game ended: "Oh, someone's unconscious. Game over."

Me, Keith, and Jody

Little Monkeys

Jody, Keith, and I were like little monkeys. We could scale up that antenna outside our house and be on the roof in two or three seconds. We would do that often if we were fighting or playing some kind of tag. When Ricky Margison was living with us, he was almost like Greg from *The Brady Bunch*—the long hair, the big collar shirt, bell bottoms, and stupid looking shoes (to us, at least). One night, Ricky was going out on a date, and being the Reeds we were, we decided we'd get up on the roof with a bucket of water, and when he came out to leave for his date, we would dump it on him. So we did. And he was *furious.* We were up there on the roof, mocking him, and he was yelling up at us—there was a tree on the other side of the house, but if he came up that way, we'd just jump off. He knew there was no way to catch us. He ended up having to go back inside and redo his hair and everything.

Ricky wasn't our only target. Some older kids who attended Horace Mann would walk through our neighborhood after school let out, to get across Parsons Avenue to Brandon High School (especially during football season to catch the games there). So we'd hide at the pond and ambush them with water balloons. They'd start chasing us, and we'd just fly past them, make it home, and scurry up onto the roof. They'd be yelling at us, "Reeds, we're gonna kill you!" But they could never catch us. We knew the area too well. The pond, Horace Mann, the orange grove—that whole little area, that was our home.

Grandpa and Grandma Reed

For a while after Jim left, there was a rift between my mom and my Reed grandparents. We didn't see Grandma and Grandpa Reed for a year or two after the divorce, even though they lived only a half mile or so away from us.

Then one day, Mom, Jody, Keith, and I were all in the car coming back from somewhere, and Mom drove past our turn onto Larson.

I remember one of us asking, "Where are you going?"

Mom just said, "It's been long enough. Let's go see your grandparents." And that was that.

From that point on, they were back in our lives—very much so. Grandma and Grandpa Reed were a huge part of my childhood. They both wore glasses. Grandma Reed had shoulder-length hair dyed dark brown, and a warm, kind smile. Grandpa had white hair, and was very quiet, but when he spoke, you listened. He tried to act hard, but he wasn't. He

Keith, when he was older, with Grandma and Grandpa Reed

taught us how to work on cars, and in the summers, he would have us do things around the house for money, like painting the house. He taught us to do things well: You did not just slap on paint. You would sand the house, prime the house, then paint it. There were no shortcuts. He instilled that in us.

Grandpa was the kind of guy who didn't believe in credit: you paid cash for what you purchased, and saved up until you could. He didn't believe in giving us money; he believed we should earn it.

Grandma Reed loved us to death. She was very outgoing and positive. She would slip us cash when Grandpa wasn't looking, and Grandpa would pretend not to know.

They were truly good people.

We would go to their house all the time, as kids, and when I got old enough to drive, I'd go over there nearly everyday. But even back in those earliest years, Mom took us to Grandpa and Grandma Reed's house often, especially for holidays. And in those early years, we were still naive enough to hope "Dad" might show up there for Thanksgiving or Christmas, or even for birthdays. Too many times, I remember us asking, "Is Dad coming? Is Dad coming?"

He never did.

Kindergarten Dropout

As a young child, I was intelligent...and stubborn. If you've ever seen *The Big Bang Theory* TV show, just picture me as a young, athletic, cute version of Sheldon Cooper. Mom sure had her hands full, raising me.

Our house was almost two miles from Yates Elementary. At six or seven years old, Mom didn't take us and drop us off at school— we rode our bikes. Today, you can't even let your kids play in the front yard without supervision. Back then, we would truck off on our bikes up the road

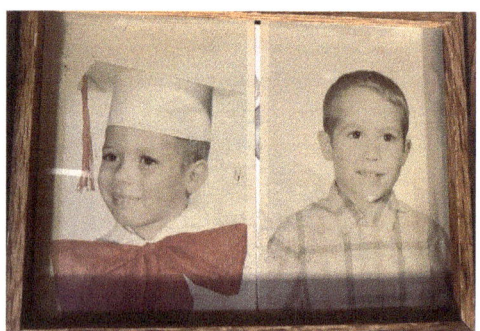

Side-by-side photos in a frame: Jody in his kindergarten graduation outfit, and me... without one.

to Jersey Avenue and down to Kingsway, go to school, and park our bikes in the bike rack. Then at the end of the day, we'd pedal away. That was just what we did.

I was a kindergarten dropout. Mom would take me to kindergarten, but I went a couple of times, and said, "These kids are stupid. I don't have time for this." I told my mom, "I'm not going anymore." (Kindergarten wasn't mandatory.) So my brother graduated from the little kindergarten, but not I.

Eventually, I started actual elementary school. When

Hairless King Arthur

At one point, Jody was in that little Kindergarten school, and they were doing a play for King Arthur. Jody, of course, was King Arthur, and he grew out his hair for *months* for the role. Right before the play, Jody decided he didn't like the long hair—it was hot or something—and he asked me to give him a haircut. I butchered it, cut all his hair off. I got my butt whipped for that one. Mom had to shave Jody's head, and he was King Arthur with no hair.

I was about six, there was a daycare center about halfway between school and our house that I was supposed to stop at on my way home. It was called Simmons Daycare—it's still there, at the time of writing this—and one day, instead of going inside, I decided, *I don't need this, I'm going home.* (Just like I'd done with kindergarten.)

Mom showed up at the daycare later to pick me up, and she was like, "Where's Paul?"

The daycare said, "He never showed up."

Mom was frantic. Kidnappings weren't part of the social norms back in the day—but still, I wasn't there.

I was home watching TV, or doing homework, or playing, or whatever.

Mom came flying into the driveway, taking the wheel sideways like *The Fast and the Furious*—and there I was, sitting on the couch, eating cereal.

Mom wasn't happy.

But I told her, just like kindergarten: "I don't think this daycare is for me."

I quit going to daycare. I remember literally thinking, "These kids are idiots. I want no part of this."

This was somewhat of a trend in my life—I've never been good at just doing what people tell me to do. As a kid, I tested quite high on my IQ test, and my national standard test results were always in the ninety-ninth percentile, so in fifth grade, the school district would have me picked up from Yates and taken to a gifted school a couple times a week... I quit that, too, because I wanted to stay and play with my friends at Yates. In my mind, those "gifted" kids at the other school were nerds, and I wanted no part of it.

When I was in school, the county bussed kids from the suburbs to the inner city, then from inner city to the suburbs. So after Yates, I was taken to a sixth-grade center, Williams, somewhere in Tampa. The next year I went to a seventh-grade center, Franklin, off I-4 near 22nd Street. We had to pick up a bus about 6 a.m. at Horace Mann. It was dark when we'd catch the bus and go to the inner city. I don't recall it being that big of an issue, didn't think much about it—we just went. Then I went to Horace Mann, and after that, I went to Brandon High.

I eventually finished school. I went to college, got my Masters, even went to law school and became a lawyer. But kindergarten or that gifted school? I couldn't be bothered.

Making Friends with Bullies

Roy Margison and I hung out a lot together, and Jody hung out a lot with a boy named Lee. Lee's dad was an architect, so they had money, but Lee was a hellion with a bit of a mean streak. He once threw a rock through a church's stained glass window, just for fun. He literally got whipped from head to toe. When we got to school the next day, the teacher asked what happened. (Remember, he was black and blue.) Lee told her. The teacher's response was, "I bet you won't do that again!"

Lee was right between Jody and me in age—I was nine, he was ten, Jody was eleven. Sometimes, I'd kind of tag along with the two of them and Lee would bust my chops and give me a hard time, but we'd still play together.

At Yates Elementary, Jody was being bullied by some bigger kid. He'd follow Jody home and mess with him. This bully was blonde-haired, pudgy, and taller than any of us.

Now, our back yard on Larson Avenue was basically a vacant lot stretching between our house and another road. There was no other house on that lot for a long time, so that was where we played baseball or football and rode our mini bikes and go-carts. The little New Hope church building was right beyond our back yard, so on Sundays, we'd get our little suits on, with our little clip-on ties, and walk to church. Beside the church building was a field, which is now apartment complexes, that stretched from New Hope Road to Clay Street. I've never seen a wheat field, but this field looked how I pictured a wheat field in my mind—it was not actual wheat, but some kind of brown straw with little feathery things up top. We had a path that cut from New Hope Road to Clay Street, because Yates Elementary was off Kingsway about a mile past Clay, so when we went to school, we'd walk through there sometimes.

Anyway, Lee and I got the idea to ambush Jody's bully in that field and beat the heck out of him. We were rednecks; we could fight. So that's exactly what we did.

I was on one side of the trail. Lee was on the other. Jody came through, and there was the bully, right behind him. When that bully got to us, he got a surprise. Jody stopped, turned around, and we all ran at him from three directions. We punched and kicked the heck out of him... but that was Brandon, back then. Fighting was a way of life. It was how we settled our differences.

Believe it or not—it's funny how this works—after that, that boy and Jody became good friends. There was no more bullying.

Chapter 2

◄─○────────────────○─►

Bunch of Hellions

The Pond

As I mentioned before, across the street from our house was a piece of land that spanned a good four to five acres, with a retention pond in the middle of it. We had a tree swing by the pond, and we had a trail there, too, a shortcut through the field that we'd use to get to Roy's house, or to Horace Mann. Cutting by the pond was quicker than going all the way down to the end of the street.

We practically lived in that pond.

The pond itself wasn't that big. It was just a pond. You could swim one side to the other, no issue, but it was nasty, so we didn't swim in it; we just played in it. We would make a ramp, and jump our bikes into it.

The pond was so nasty, at some point it caused an infection in my ear that lasted for about a year. My ear would clog, and I'd have to go to the doctor, and he'd suction out what looked like a raw oyster out of my ear. But it felt so good when it came out. Then he'd put the medicine in, and say "Stay out of the pond." But we weren't gonna stay out of the pond—it was the pond. Between doctor visits, if my ear was hurting me, Mom would blow a little cigarette smoke into my ear to help soothe it. Eventually, I got immune to it or something, because the infection went away—or maybe we just quit riding our bikes into the pond.

The Guys

We had a great group of kids in the neighborhood. Like I said, our group was mostly boys... there were a couple of girls, but they were older, and we were hellions so they didn't want to hang out with us.

As I mentioned earlier, Horace Mann Middle School used to be our playground. The north end of the school was a long hallway. It started level, then went down, got flat for a bit, went down a little more by the office, went flat for a bit, then went down again and ended by the girl's locker room. We would get dish soap, put water near the end where the girls' locker room was, and start hauling butt down from the north end. The goal was to slide your bike and wipe out when you got to the soap, to see who could get closest to the wall without hitting it. Sometimes, if we went too fast, there would be horrific crashes into that cement wall. Once somebody got seriously hurt, that was how the game ended.

We'd play chase with bikes at Horace Mann, too. The rule was that you had to make contact to tag someone, but there were blind spots at the turns, so sometimes you'd be speeding away on your bike from one guy while another person might be coming around the corner. Sometimes there'd be horrific crashes that way. If a crash caused significant injury—which some did, there were broken bones—that's when the game would end. One time, it was one of the Margison brothers. He was older, and we were running from him. When he went to tag Lee, he crashed into one of the metal poles holding up the roof, and broke his collarbone. That ended the game.

Of course, we couldn't let our parents know about the injuries, or we'd get our butts whipped—"Why were you doing *that*?!"—so we hid the injuries as best we could. With the bicycle injuries, usually nothing much was broken, but occasionally we thought we may have cracked some ribs. Again, we couldn't tell anybody, because we'd get in trouble.

Then there was skateboarding. In the summer, we skateboarded down Lakewood Drive. It has this huge, long hill in the road. It's a busy road today, but back then, there were hardly any cars. We'd walk with our skateboards from Larson over to Lakewood, and we'd skateboard all day. If we put two skateboards side by side, we could double skateboard. We could go faster that way, because with singles, if you're going too fast, the board would start to shake.

There were some bad crashes, as you can imagine—it's a big hill, and we were flying down, so if we hit a pebble... We would try to make sure the road was clean, but there were some wipeouts with significant bleeding. There were no elbow pads back then, no gloves, and no one wore helmets. More than likely it was shorts and a t-shirt because it was summer time. We got our share of road rash.

> **The Mom Pitch**
>
> We didn't have cell phones back then, but we lived close, so when it was getting late, we'd hear Mom: "Jody! Paul! Keith!" That's how we knew it was time to come home. Mom would just go out in the yard and scream.
> Sometimes she'd call, usually for dinner, and we'd hear her but not go. We could hear the pitch – that mom pitch – and finally when the pitch got to the level that we were going to die, we would go home, and get our butt whippin' because she'd be frothed at the mouth by then. But hey, we were playing football, and the game was tied—we couldn't just go home.

The swing by the pond was another of our pastimes. Sometimes, we'd try to put nearly everyone we knew on the swing at once. The swing would come back, and another person would jump on. One day, this girl named Kim was the first one on. (God bless country girls, love 'em to death.) The swing broke, and she was on the bottom. She was injured. I don't remember how badly, but it was ugly.

Then there were the firecracker wars. This one time, a group was on one side, and Jody and Roy were over on the other side. Roy had a firecracker in his hand. Jody lit the firecracker, but Roy didn't know it. *Boom!* It blew up in his hand. We thought it was the funniest thing we'd ever seen in our life. Roy, not so much. He still talks about that: "Remember that firecracker? You nearly blew off my hand!" That was near the pond, another pond incident.

Our other big pastime at the pond was BB gun wars with our air Daisies. The rule was that you had to shoot somebody below the waist. But freakin' Lee came with his pump BB Gun.

We were like, "You ain't shooting us with that!'

I love Lee, but as I mentioned, he was mean as heck. He said, "I'll only pump it once."

Now, mind you, even one pump was still twice as strong as a little air Daisy. And if we hit Lee, we could hear him cock it twice.

We'd shout, "Lee! You can't shoot us with that!"

As usual, we played until somebody got hurt, then the game was over. One time a BB got me right under the eye. Thankfully, it didn't put my eye out.

We didn't tell our parents about *any* of these injuries, because we'd get a butt whippin': "What're you doing having BB gun fights?!" So the injuries had to be concealed. We'd wear baggy sweatshirts and pretend to be cold when asked, "Aren't you hot? It's ninety degrees outside!" so that our parents wouldn't ask where we got the bruises.

Not all injuries could be hidden. One time we were playing baseball and the ball went down in the sewer. It wasn't like we had a dozen balls; we had one ball and one bat. We had to get the ball out. It was raining, but we often played in the rain. We lifted the manhole cover and it slipped. I dropped it and broke my foot. That one was hard to hide.

And then there was the time we were on the go-carts and Lee's hat flew off. He reached under the tire to get it, but it was an old road that

---

We Weren't the Only Hellions

One Halloween night, we were walking on the sidewalk from our house on Parsons and some kids came by in a car, screaming and hollering.

Next thing we knew, Keith was like, "They just threw something at me!"

It was a pool ball. It went in his jacket, but if it had hit him, it could've killed him. They just threw it at him, flying by. That's how things were in Brandon back then.

---

had rock in the cement—the good kind of road that has no potholes, that you could drop a bomb on and it would still be there. But Lee's hand got stuck, and it was just dragging along the road, and he was screaming, but of course he couldn't pull it out until we stopped. We were in a two-seater, so when we stopped, I got out and Lee pulled his hand out. He'd peeled the skin off. It looked like Skeletor. I was freaking out.

But Lee just said, "I'll walk home, just go home!"

Injuries were just a part of life, back then, but it could've been far worse.

Classic Reed Maneuver

Remember that field I mentioned, the one with the trail from New Hope Road to Clay? Well, one day, we had the bright idea to set that field on fire so the fireman would come. Mind you, the fireman in Brandon back then was like Barney Fife. He had an old fire truck, with a little old hose that he unwound. It wasn't like the big fire trucks we have today. We just liked watching him do it.

Of course, when he showed up, we helped him put out the fire—that was a classic Reed maneuver, helping put out the fire that we started. And he was really thankful that we helped him!

You'd think we would've gotten snake-bitten a lot more than we did or gotten injured a lot more than we did. We dodged a lot of bullets with injuries. I don't pretend to understand how guardian angels work, but if we had them, we surely kept ours busy.

Protecting Our Pond

At the pond, we had a tree fort.

Growing up, Grandma and Grandpa Reed had some money. And so every Christmas, whatever else we got, there would be a bicycle for each one of us. And hey, as long as you got a bike for Christmas, who cared if the only other stuff you got was underwear and socks? You got a bike.

So one year, Lee got a bike, I got a bike, and Jody got a bike. We parked them under this huge oak tree near the pond. We were

CHAPTER
TWO

probably like eight, nine, and ten years old—pretty little. We were up in the tree. Now, remember, Lee was mean as heck, but I still love him to death.

Three older girls came by, just these mean redneck girls we didn't know, and they were really acting nasty to us.

So we were like, "Who are you? What are you doing here? This is *our* pond."

And they said, "Whatever. Come down here, and we'll beat you up!"

I don't remember what else was said, but one of them was smoking. Lee's bike was down below, and she put her cigarette out on his seat and burned a hole in it.

Well, you'd have thought Lee was a monkey. He *flew* down out of that tree, grabbed a rock, and pelted her right in the face. Now, I'm not saying it was right—but it's what happened.

So Jody and I were like, "Ohhhh!"

And the girl was bleeding, crying, and screaming.

We thought we were in a lot of trouble, but we never heard from them and they never came back.

Back in the day, stuff like that happened. We did a lot of protecting our home.

"Reeds, I Know It's You!"

There were only one or two cops in Brandon when we were teenagers, and Steve was one of them. He was a little older than us, and he became a cop.

Sometimes, Jody and Keith and I would go into the orange groves, pick some oranges, and when cars would go by on Kingsway, we'd orange-bomb them. No cars could turn back and chase us, because the sand in the orange groves was two or three inches deep.

So one time, Steve drove by in his cop car—and Jody blasted him with the oranges.

Steve slammed on the brakes, spun back, and tried to chase us through the orange groves. But of course, he got stuck.

He was yelling, "Reeds! I know it's you!"

Perry Mason and Major League Baseball

Someone once asked me, "What made you want to become a lawyer? When did you first think about that?"

Honestly, it all goes back to Perry Mason.

I went to Horace Mann for eighth and ninth grade. Back then, if you lived close enough, you could walk home for lunch. Horace Mann wasn't air conditioned. It was hot. So I would go home for lunch, and just not go back to school in the afternoon to avoid the heat. I watched Archie Bunker, the Jeffersons, and Perry Mason. Then two o'clock came, and Jody and Keith would come home.

But Perry Mason made me fascinated by the law. That's what started it. There was no follow up; I didn't take classes, or prepare for it or anything—as a redneck from Brandon, I thought my destiny was playing Major League Baseball. That was the goal, and my brother Jody and I were both pretty good at it. (He did play MLB for eleven years.) I was heading that direction, college ball and all, but I blew out my shoulder and so be it—that's just the way it goes. So I majored in Physical Education, and thought I'd teach high school sports or something.

Who would ever expect a redneck, kindergarten dropout from Brandon to become a successful lawyer? Certainly not me.

But this was our home. So we flew through the orange groves, came out the other side on South Valrico, ran around, and went through Clay Street. (Back then, there was no body fat on any of us, with all the bicycling and running and playing.) Then we circled back like a military maneuver, fifteen to twenty minutes later, and watched him still trying to get his car out of the sand.

What Rednecks Did in Brandon on a Friday or Saturday Night

When I got to be thirteen, fourteen, fifteen, and some of the older guys in our group could drive, Friday or Saturday nights were for egg wars.

Gary (he was sixteen) had a big ol' tank of a car. I don't even know what it was, but it was huge. Jody's friend Steve had a Volkswagon and someone else had a Chevy Corvair. Jody wrecked a lot of cars, so it's hard to say what he had at the time, but it was probably a Mustang or a

Nova.

We'd go to the Albertson's or a couple of different stores, and literally buy all the eggs they had. Then we'd draw up a little map of the area where we could drive our cars—from North Brandon into Seffner, but we had to stay between Kingsway and Parsons and Wheeler and Clay Street. We knew the area.

We would drive around, and when we saw one of the four cars, it was game on with the egg war. We'd go by like knights with chariot sticks, and we'd just blast 'em. We'd be hanging out of windows: "Oh I'm hit!" *Bam!* In the forehead, the chest, whatever.

There was no alcohol, no drugs— just fun! This was Brandon, and it was just what we did on the weekend.

Ramada Inn and John

At the intersection of State Road 60 and U.S. 301 on the west edge of Brandon, there was a Ramada Inn. Mom, Jody, Keith, and I used it as our swimming pool. We'd act like we had a room, and go swimming. Mom was very attractive, and the hotel manager didn't really care if Barbara Ann and the kids swam in the pool. I remember him coming out and chatting her up.

That's also where Mom met one of my step-dads, the first one who stuck around—John Morrell. He was staying at the hotel.

John was a good-looking man. He was big and muscular, about six feet tall, dark-haired, Italian, and a stud, with a '65 or '66 Corvette convertible. He worked for what used to be IMC Phosphate, the phosphate mines out in Polk County, before they got bought out by Mosaic. They had these drag lines with huge cranes, as big as your house, to scoop up dirt. John was a mechanic; he worked on the cranes. He worked all hours—if it broke down, they'd call him, even in the middle of the night. He made good money.

John came into the picture when I was around ten or eleven, and he coached me in Pony League when I was thirteen. He was a nice guy and he was in the picture for about four years, until I was about fourteen.

John and his brother Roger also owned Breezemaker Fans in Tampa & Ybor City, a family company they inherited. After the A/C was put into the house on Larson, the living room and the kitchen near the garage were comfortable. But the bedrooms were on the opposite side of the house, and in the heat of summer, there was only so much that old wall unit could do. The master bedroom was all the way down the hallway to the right, with its own bathroom, and the other two bedrooms were on the left, with the other bathroom across from them. There was an entrance to the attic in the hall where the bedrooms were. So John cut a big hole right up into the attic and put a huge industrial fan in there. When he turned it on, it would make a loud noise—I mean, it was like starting up a jet engine or something—but it pulled the air through the house, and dropped the temperature in those bedrooms probably twenty degrees. You could feel the cool air coming down the hallway. I don't know if that fan's still there, but we were sure glad to have it.

Even after John and Mom split, I stayed in touch with him for a long time. As adults, we'd go out and drink some beers when he got off work. I haven't seen him in a while. I don't know if he's even still alive. But John and Stinger were the closest things I had to dads. And of course, Stinger was Stinger. He was a great guy, and he deserves a section of his own. But he didn't come into the picture until I was in college. For the seven years in between John and Stinger, there was no dad.

Done with Whoopins

My Nana, my mom's mom, was a drunk. There's really no other way to say it. She'd come over to help cook or whatever on the weekends, but inevitably, she'd start beating on Mom. So we'd go running in our pajamas to Ms. Linda's, which was three houses down. Then Mom would come running down, and we'd wait for Nana to leave. That happened often.

But Nana put Mom through nursing school and felt the need to do whatever she wanted to do.

Luckily, Nana found the Lord and all that stopped.

And it also stopped because, eventually, we got big enough to say, "Hey, I think we're done with you beatin' on Mom."

We used to get butt-whoopins with the belt, too, so that also stopped around the same time... We told Mom, "No, we're good. We're done with whoopins."

Still Can't Sleep Without a Fan

Pre-air conditioning on Larson Avenue, the house windows just stayed open and everybody had a fan. To this day, in my mom's house, my house, and my kids' houses, you will find a fan in every room. In Mom's house, they're mounted on the wall. Mine is in the corner of my bedroom. My daughter LeeAnn has one in hers. We just can't sleep without the noise of a fan, because we grew up with it.

When I was playing baseball at Brandon High School, I'd go home to take a nap between school and practice. I didn't have an alarm clock, but the fan had a one-hour timer. So I'd set the timer, go to sleep, and when the fan clicked off, I'd wake up.

To this day, if I'm sleeping and the electricity goes out, the fan cutting off wakes me up, and it's the same with LeeAnn. LeeAnn's bedroom and my bedroom are on opposite sides of the house. One night, the power went out and we met in the middle— we'd both gotten up to see what happened.

When I traveled, if the hotel didn't have a fan, I'd just have to go buy one.

LeeAnn and I went snow skiing once, and we stopped at Walmart on the way to get a fan. The store clerk was dumbfounded. Finally, she understood what we were asking for and took us to the shelf. There was one box fan, and it was pink. But I was like, "I don't care. It's a fan!" The lady was probably thinking, *These people from Florida are crazy!*

These days, I use an app on my phone that has "bedtime fan" sounds, so that I can sleep. Ryan and I recently went to Reno, and we shared a hotel room. I put my phone on the table between the beds with the fan app running, but I forgot to plug in my phone. Around 4 in the morning, my phone died, and Ryan and I both woke up.

Ryan was like, "What happened?"

I said, "I don't know, I guess my phone died." I plugged it back in and turned on the app, and we were right back to sleep.

Burgers, Fried Potatoes, and a Hershey Bar

Grandma and Grandpa Reed had some kind of mineral mine in Ohio, and he was in the oil business. You wouldn't know it from their small house on Rosier Road, but as I mentioned, they had money, and if Grandpa wanted a car, he paid cash. He didn't believe in credit. Grandma sold Tupperware. She was a Tupperware machine; she'd earn a free car every year. They weren't Kardashians or anything like that, but if we wanted or needed something, they could give it to us.

When I turned sixteen, I got a car, a '67 Camaro. It had no air conditioning, no heater, and no power steering. Back then, high school was grades ten, eleven, and twelve. I made the baseball team as a sophomore, but Brandon High was on double sessions, and I went in the mornings, so I had a gap between school and practice. Since I had my own car, I'd drive to Grandma's when I got out of school at noon, and she would cook me a hamburger with a potato that she would cut up into homestyle fries. I couldn't drink with my meal—that was one of Grandpa's rules, it slowed digestion—so I'd have to wait to drink water. And every single time, Grandma would give me a Hershey's chocolate bar for dessert, along with cash, like $20, and she'd say, "Don't tell your grandpa."

Twenty bucks, back then, when gas cost less than a dollar? I was in hog heaven.

I'd watch *As the World Turns* with her, or *All My Children*. Nearly every day after school, I would go to visit Grandma—get a hamburger with no bun, cut up potatoes, a Hershey bar, a glass of water, and watch a little TV. Then I'd go to baseball practice, or if it wasn't baseball season, I'd go find something to do.

Once a year, Grandpa wanted to paint his house. So when Keith was younger, Jody and I would go over there. As I mentioned, he'd make us scrape the wood, prime it, paint it... then at the end of the day, Grandpa would pay us some money.

If we ever had problems with our cars, Grandpa was old-school: you fixed it yourself. So we wouldn't go to a mechanic, we'd call Grandpa. And he could do it, but he'd make *us* do it.

One time I dropped a little bolt in the manifold of the carburetor. We had to get it out, because if we cranked the car it would ruin the engine. We spent two hours trying to get it out. Grandpa taped a magnet onto a metal clothes hanger, and we tried to get it down inside the engine to grab the bolt. Both of us were about at the end of our rope. Finally, after a couple of hours (thank the Lord Jesus above), literally on our last try, just when we were about to give up, we pulled it out and there was that bolt, stuck to the magnet. If that hadn't worked, Grandpa would've made me take apart that whole engine and rebuild it.

I may not have had a silver spoon growing up, but I had my friends, I had my family—I had a hamburger, fried potatoes, and a Hershey bar.

I had everything I needed.

Chapter 3

***

Not Gonna Happen

College Ball

After I graduated high school, I went to Manatee Junior College on a baseball scholarship. I also got scholarship offers to Florida State and Mississippi State, and looking back I probably should have gone to one of those, but I just didn't. I was pretty sure Florida State only wanted me because they wanted Jody to come back for his senior year, rather than signing the deal he'd been offered with the Tigers. And as for Mississippi—I was a Mama's boy, I'd never left Brandon. To me, even Manatee seemed far; it was more than an hour away from home. But Jody had played there for two years after high school, so I just followed his footsteps. I went up and played summer ball for Florida State, but enrolled to attend Manatee for my first college semester.

The coach who was at Manatee when I arrived was a different coach than the one who had recruited Jody, and the new coach hadn't liked Jody—so right off the bat, he didn't like me. Basically, he was a jerk. I played baseball there and attended Manatee for one semester, then decided to leave.

The next logical choice would have been Hillsborough Community College (HCC), back near Brandon, but for some reason I didn't want to go there—I don't remember why. However, I heard about this small, private college in Temple Terrace, only about twenty minutes from home: Florida College (FC). I called the baseball coach and said, "I want to play here."

And he said, "Who the heck are you?"

I told him to call my high school coach for a reference, and I guess he did and that my coach said, "Yeah, you want him," because he called me back and offered me a scholarship to come play baseball. I was very skilled, and my reputation must have preceded me, because when the second baseman at FC at the time found out I was transferring in, he immediately transferred to HCC—he knew I'd be taking his position.

So in 1982, I started at FC on a baseball scholarship, and I got a Pell Grant for whatever that didn't cover. I didn't live on campus like most of the students; I lived at home, and drove to campus for class and practices.

FC is a religious school. Back then, no one could wear shorts, and the girls couldn't even wear pants until maybe after hours or something. There were certainly no co-ed dorms, and every student had to take Bible classes. We went to church growing up, so it's not like I didn't know the basics, but when I was in Freshman Bible at FC, my classmates may as well have been the twelve disciples. They were talking, asking questions, and I was like, "This is all new!" I felt like I was the idiot sitting at the Vatican surrounded by the Pope and a bunch of cardinals. I really tried, but it was like they were doing advanced Bible calculus while I was still adding and subtracting. Finally, after getting twenties and the like on the tests, about halfway through the course I realized there was no way that I could pass. So I quit going to class.

One day I saw the professor in the hall, and he asked me, "You planning on coming to class?" (He was kind about it. They were all really nice people there.)

I said, "Why? I can't pass."

He said, sympathetically, "Well, yes, you have kind of dug yourself in a hole."

I replied, "It's more like a crater."

We both laughed, and he went on his way. I never went back to class—and he never said anything more about it. Needless to say, I got the first F in my life in that class.

I needed a certain number of credit hours to qualify to play baseball. I'd only brought twelve credit hours with me from Manatee, and then that first semester at FC, I screwed up my credits pretty badly. Suddenly, my sophomore year, I was far behind.

I also knew that an AA degree from FC would transfer to another university, but if I didn't finish my AA, 99 percent of the classes wouldn't transfer because they were special religious classes. I needed to finish my AA there. So I played baseball in the fall, sixty games, and I took eighteen hours that semester. Some were religious classes—one credit hour of the book of John or something, two credit hours of Corinthians—and then the usual college classes. The next semester, I was *really* in trouble. I needed to cram in twenty-one credit hours. I had to get special permission from the Dean.

He called me into his office: "Do you think you can do this?"

I told him, "I don't have a choice."

So he approved it, and believe it or not, I pulled it off. I completed my sophomore year at FC and finished my AA degree. I'm still in touch with some of my teammates from FC baseball today, and they'll tell me, "Dude, that's all you did. You were playing baseball, or you were in the library."

But it's always been that way with me: once I set my mind to do something, nothing can stop me.

I made a lot of good friends at FC who are still my friends today. In fact, I met Bob Wellon there, who's now a CPA and a vital part of how Reed & Reed began... but I'll get to that later. For now, suffice it to say he's still a close friend, and we still go out to lunch together once every few months. FC was also where I met Jim Roberts, who's now an assistant state attorney. He played at Hillsborough High School (about thirty minutes from Brandon) before playing for FC. Up until Covid hit in 2020, Jim and I were still meeting once a week or so for lunch. Most of my buddies from the FC baseball team lived off campus like I did, except the ones who'd come to FC from out of state. David Patterson, from Massachusetts, was a bit of a hellion like me. He stayed with me more or less every weekend, because if not, he'd probably have gotten kicked out of FC for the partying he liked to do on the weekends.

I had actually injured my shoulder my senior year of high

school, but I managed to keep playing with the injury through my two years at FC. My family didn't have much money, so having surgery and then rehabbing for a year or two just wasn't an option back then. I just kept playing with the pain. By my second year at FC, I was taking so much ibuprofen and acetaminophen that I was vomiting up blood.

I played second base, so if I had to turn a double play where I needed to gun the ball, I couldn't use my arm for probably ten minutes afterward. There were times when I'd gun somebody out, and when I had to bat after that, I couldn't swing. Coach knew, so I would just hold the bat, and if I got four balls, I would walk; or if I struck out, I'd go back to the dugout. If I could move my arm, I'd try to base hit bunt. I got really good at base hit bunts. But my injury just kept getting worse and worse. Eventually, the pain got so bad I couldn't even wipe my own butt.

I got a scholarship to play ball at a school in North Carolina, but by that point, the pain was such that it affected every single day of my life. I took the train up to North Carolina, met the coach, took the tour, all that, then came back home and realized... I can't do this. I called the coach: "I'm not coming." I just couldn't keep living with that kind of pain. I was done.

Baseball players make a lot of money—it's a great life. But it's also a grind. I saw it with Jody: he played eleven years, but every single year, when he'd come home in the off-season, he'd say he was done. When he started each season, he'd weigh around 165-170 pounds, and by the time he came home, he'd weigh maybe 150. People don't realize how grueling professional sports can be. It didn't surprise me when Tom Brady announced his retirement in February of 2022... but I said when he did it, "He's gonna go home, play with the family, then get stir crazy and go back. It's in his blood." (I was right.) And it was the same with Jody. He got five to six months off every year, so when he ended each season he'd swear it was his last, but by spring training, he was ready to go back... until he just wasn't. Jody could've played one more year for the Tigers, made an extra million or two, but he said, "Nah, I'm done," for real that time.

Baseball is a grind, mentally and physically—and by that second year of playing with my injury, I knew it was my time to quit. It wasn't a devastating decision, not like people imagine it might've been. As much as I loved baseball, the pain had gotten so bad that getting out of it was like a breath of fresh air. It was time to move on; my baseball career was over.

At that point, I announced to my mom that I was going to the University of South Florida (USF) to major in Physical Education. My plan was to teach high school P.E. and coach high school baseball. Mom wasn't thrilled about my sudden change of life plans, but what could she do? It's not like the Major League was in the cards for me, anymore. USF was a good school, and it was near home—simple as that. The campus was about twenty-five minutes from our house in Brandon. So I went on to USF, and I graduated with my Bachelors in Physical Education in 1986.

Stinger

Jody got drafted to the Major Leagues in 1984. In 1985, he played in Winter Haven. That's when Stinger came in.

Mom met Stinger when she and Jody were living in Winter Haven. Jody was still in Single-A at the time, and I was right around twenty years old, close to graduating with my Bachelors from USF. Stinger was coaching for the Red Sox; he saw Mom in the stands... and that was that. Stinger was around for nearly thirty years. He even helped me pay for law school. He called me Junior. He had his own biological kids, but we were always very close.

At Stinger's forty-year reunion for the Red Sox, we pulled up into the limo line at the fancy hotel the team provided,

Stinger, in 2009.

riding in a rickshaw. We got crazy looks, but Stinger just said, "It was Junior's idea."

There was a special shirt presented to Stinger at that re-union—his old number. He took me aside and told me, "Junior, I really wish I could give you this shirt, but I need to give it to my son." I understood completely, but he just wanted me to know.

I last saw Stinger a couple years ago. He was dying. He had dementia. We drank one last beer together while Mom was out; she needed a break. He passed a few days later. That was the best beer I ever had.

Stinger was the closest thing I ever had to a real dad. I loved that man!

Keith Interlude #1: The Brawl on 92

(A note about Keith: My brother Keith did a lot of crazy things... and often, I'd get roped in somehow. So I have a lot of Keith stories. I've picked just a few to share in this book, ones that relate to other things I've mentioned, or that just really highlight the kind of chaotic adventures that came from being Keith's brother. Keith was loyal to no end, with a heart of gold, and clever as a snake... but he was also Keith. You'll see what I mean.)

One time, my brother Keith, his friend Smitty, and I were on our way back from visiting Mom and Stinger in Winter Haven. We were coming off of I-4, south on County Road 579. We stopped at a red light near a Shell gas station with a Hardee's across the street, at the intersection of 579 and Highway 92. Somebody honked at somebody, and next thing I knew, the guy in front of us was getting out of his car.

So Keith and I got out of the car, too, and Smitty stayed in the back seat.

The guy from the other car came up and got right in my face.

Well, you just didn't threaten someone Keith cared about. Keith belted the guy right upside the head.

So of course the guy turned toward Keith, fuming. He was gonna hit Keith, for sure, so as soon as he turned, *boom*, I smoked him, too, before he even had the chance.

So then the guy spun back toward me—Keith whacked him again.

I mean, really, this guy couldn't be all that bright if he hadn't figured out what to expect by now.

Suddenly, Smitty yelled, "Light's green! We gotta go!"

Keith and I jumped back in, and we took off.

I don't know if you've had the pleasure of being in a fight, but you win some and you lose some. The thing is, when you lose one, you don't feel like a man. So that guy got his ego hurt, because he lost the fight, and he just wouldn't let it go. Next thing we knew, the guy was trying to ram his car into the back of ours.

We were flying down those back roads, going about a hundred miles per hour, trying to outrun this guy, until we finally managed to lose him.

Life with Keith was certainly never boring.

Keith Interlude #2: Why Mom Moved to Melbourne

When Mom lived in Winter Haven with Stinger, Keith and I (and sometimes Smitty) would go visit and play golf.

One day, we were out playing golf, and Keith did something that angered me. I don't remember what it was, but for whatever reason, I wouldn't let it go, and he was running his mouth.

Toward the end of the round, there was this twenty-foot hill on the side of the golf course. The way it was configured, you couldn't really see what was on the top of the hill unless you were paying attention.

Smitty was driving Keith's cart, and I was up on the hill.

I sped down the hill and rammed into the side of their cart.

It flipped them over.

Of course, the cart was trashed. We had to leave it.

Now, that golf course writes down the number of the golf cart you're taking—we're probably the reason why! Because they were like, "We know it was you."

And Mom said, "How do you know? You can't prove it was them. We're not paying for it."

So now they write down your number.

But that was one of many times that Keith and I dragged Mom in on our trouble—I don't know if that was actually the one that pushed Mom another 180 miles away to Melbourne, or not... but it was pretty funny.

Marriage and a Murder

I got married at a young age—twenty-one or twenty-two— right around when I graduated college. Her name was Kathy. We met in 1986, soon before I got my BA. She was beautiful and nice. We started dating, then broke up, reconnected briefly, then broke up again... and a month later I found out she was pregnant.

So I asked her to marry me. I was a redneck—in my mind, if you got a girl pregnant, you married her. That's just what you did. And nobody else seemed to think otherwise. So we planned a wedding. And for the first few years, things were great. We were in love, and I was excited to be a father, despite the surprise circumstances.

Kathy and I moved into what seemed like a nice apartment in Temple Terrace on the river, just across from King High School's baseball field. I'd gotten a job at the USF Psychiatry Center from 8 a.m. to 5 p.m., teaching and assisting with the children and adolescents, then I worked nights at the Tampa Tribune, loading papers onto trucks for $5 an hour. I'd come home about midnight. That was our life for the next few months.

On August 8, 1987, Ryan was born.

I've already said I was excited to become a father... but of course, I was also scared. Becoming a parent is a crazy experience. You don't know what you're doing. You just go to the hospital, and a day later they hand you a baby and say, "Good luck!"

Ryan's situation was a little different—he was premature, born a month early, and he only weighed four plus pounds. He was in the NICU incubator for a month, and we'd go every day to see him. I was excited to have a son, and that never changed with any of my kids—I didn't care how young or old I was, or what the circumstances, or if they were a boy or a girl, I was excited for every single one of them. Scared... *terrified*... but excited.

When I first met Ryan, he was tiny. They wrapped him in that little white blanket with the blue stripes, and I was like, "Holy crap!" He was barely bigger than my current cell phone. Because he was born so early, there were concerns. When we finally got to take him home, it was brutal. My mom was a nurse, so she brought us those little bottles of liquid Enfamil, which was good. Every two hours, we had to give Ryan an eyedropper-full of formula. If he drank more than that, great, but he had to drink at least that much, and no one went back to bed until it was gone. So one of us might be up for an hour trying to get him to drink, rubbing him, frustrated, tired, muttering "Come on!" Kathy and I took turns doing that, and I also went to work.

After working the day at the Psychiatry Center and until about midnight at the Tampa Tribune, I would come home and still need to help Kathy with Ryan so that she could rest. I'd get a couple hours of sleep here or there, at best. Thankfully, I've never been a big eight-hour sleeper, so sleep itself wasn't as big of a struggle for me as it was for Kathy. I wasn't really that sleepy, I was just *tired* from working and doing so much. Still, it was hard for the first few months. After that, Ryan started taking a bottle, and it got easier. When he got a bit older, Mom and Stinger would take Ryan as much as we wanted them to, and so would Mimi and Poppy (Kathy's parents). It was a community effort, for sure. But those first three or four months after he first came home were like hell—just exhausting.

Becoming a father changed me. Before that, I was a wild dog. Drinking,

> **Stacking the Alarms**
> Growing up, I was never a big sleeper, but I hated waking up to an alarm, so I created a way to make it less miserable. I went to bed at 9 or 10 p.m. as a kid, and I would set my alarm clock for midnight or 1 a.m. to wake me up so I could say, "Oh man, I get five more hours to sleep!" Then I'd reset the clock for 4 a.m., and when it went off I'd be like, "I get three more hours!" And so on. If I somehow missed one of the alarms and slept until it was actually time to get up, I'd wake up all angry. I'm still that way today— just the other day, I slept through one of my earlier alarms, and woke up just in time to get ready... I was pissed!

partying... all that started in high school. But now, I had a responsibility. In 1988, my job at USF offered to pay for me to get my Masters, so I returned to USF for a Masters in Special Education and Behavior Disorders. At one point, I was working 8 a.m. to 5 p.m. at the Psychiatry Center then 7 p.m. to 11 p.m. at the Tampa Tribune on Mondays, Wednesdays, and Fridays, plus taking my Masters classes on Tuesdays and Thursdays, and working Saturdays and Sundays at the Tribune. You only do that if you have responsibilities. None of it was handed to me. I worked to take care of my family.

As I said, at first we lived in that little apartment near King High School. A little old lady lived below us, but we didn't really know her. We hadn't lived there that long.

Around two or three in the morning one night, we woke up with police lights flashing everywhere. There was a knock on the door—it was Officer Steve, what were the odds of that? He was a detective now. Only because he knew us, he told us the old lady had been murdered.

We were young, Ryan was a baby—we were freaking out. Did people just get *murdered* in this place? How often did that happen? Would the murderer come back?

There was an investigation, the police staked things out... We were even on the news; they came out and interviewed us as the victim's neighbors. Eventually, they discovered it was the old lady's son who had killed her. But in the meantime, Kathy and I were like, "We gotta get the heck out of here."

We moved out of that apartment, and into a double-wide trailer in Davpam Mobile Home Community.

Keith Interlude #3: Keith Reed, Hero

While I was in the hospital with Kathy and little Ryan-to-be on the night of Ryan's birth, there was a hellacious storm in Brandon that evening.

There's a pretty big pond off of Highway 60 near the Dunkin' Donuts, and apparently a woman lost control and went off the road into the pond during the storm. Her car sank to the bottom of this pond that was ten to fifteen feet deep.

Good ol' Keith pulled over, jumped in, and saved the woman.

He got an award from the mayor, it was on TV, the whole works.

He cut out the newspaper article and had it in his house, on the wall near the kitchen: "Keith Reed, Hero." Keith was super proud of it, but for whatever reason, I didn't notice until much later that the date of the event was 8-8-87. The night Ryan was born.

That's the kind of guy Keith was—if someone went into a pond, he was jumping in to save their life. He'd give you the shirt off his back... or he'd beat the hell out of you. It could go either way. I used to say Keith had a big heart and a small mind. His nickname was Moreeder. Why, you ask? Because everybody needs a little *more* Keith Reed.

Moreeder, we love and miss you every day!

Davpam and a Tonka Truck

We lived in Davpam Mobile Home Park for a few years, after we moved out of that murder apartment. Davpam is still there, and people don't believe me now when I say I used to live there. Not that I'm criticizing Davpam. It was a nice place to live, and it was what we could afford. But it's been there a long time, and it's not where most think I would have ever lived. Whatever you see me with today, it was by the grace of God and from hard work and perseverance. Because, believe me, I didn't start where I am now. I started from scratch.

One year, while we lived at Davpam, someone got Ryan one of those electric Tonka trucks for Christmas, the ones kids can ride on. He might have been three or four years old. There was this huge dirt hill outside the mobile home park, and Ryan just insisted I was to take his truck to the top of that hill so he could ride it down. I'm talking like a twenty-foot-high sand hill.

Everyone was against it.

Ryan is pig-headed and stubborn even now, and as a little three or four year old, he was no different. He pitched a fit—"I can do this!"—until finally, I toted him up with his truck.

I said, "Junior, this is a huge mistake."

And he looked right at me and said, "I got this."

Have you seen those ski crashes on Wide World of Sports with the skier coming down the slope and crashing head-over-heels at the end? Well, that's exactly what Ryan did as soon as he came over the edge of that slope. He was ass over el-

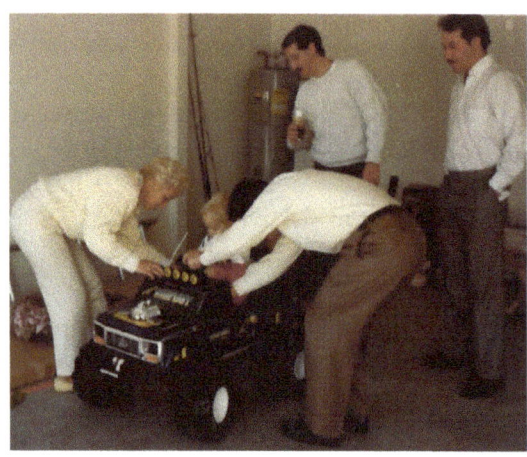

Ryan on the Tonka Truck

bows, all the way down. It ruined his brand new truck.

Luckily he wasn't seriously hurt, no hospitalization required—but that was the funniest thing I'd ever seen. That would've been a YouTube/TikTok gone viral if I've ever seen one. (Actually, it probably would've been me going to jail for reckless endangerment of the kids.)

But you couldn't tell Ryan *no* on some things. So it was, "Yeah, you wanna go do it? Do it." And he'd learn.

He only did it once.

Our family soon grew. Our daughter Brittany was born in 1991, while we still lived in that mobile home. About a year later, my brother Jody bought us a house, and we moved our little family out of Davpam. I guess that's just what family does for one another.

Hasta la Vista

Unfortunately, my marriage to Kathy didn't last long after Brittany was born. Things that year hadn't been going well between us. Like many who get married at a young age, we struggled to grow up without growing apart. For us, it just didn't happen.

I'm 0 for 2 on marriages at this point, and I'm not just going to blame the ex-wives. I played a part in each of them. I was young, immature, and I got irritated over a lot of little things that I could've shrugged off. I doubt very seriously if I'll ever get married again, but I'm sure I would be a better husband today than I was back then. I've learned a lot since those days.

Ryan, me, Brittany, and Mom in Jody's pool (You can also see Jody's dog, Ally, swimming there behind me.)

It was around March of 1992 when Kathy told me she wanted a divorce. Ryan was four; Brittany was eighteen months. Within three months of Kathy, Ryan, Brittany, and I moving into the house Jody bought us, I got the proverbial boot out of the house. I laugh now, but back then, it was not that funny.

I didn't put up a fuss. I remember I had packed up to leave,

Mom, Brittany, me, and Ally (Jody's dog) in Jody's pool

and there was a babysitter there, a teenager, probably around fifteen or sixteen years old, who regularly babysat for us. Kathy had left for something, and I was getting the last of my stuff. Ryan and Brittany were crying, and I was trying not to. The babysitter was like, "Paul, it'll be alright."

I gave Ryan and Brittany a hug, and told them, "I'll be just around the corner. It'll be okay."

I was crying, the babysitter was crying—it was a rough day.

Around that time, Jody was heading to Boston for the start of the Major League season, which begins in April. He had a house in New Tampa with a German shepherd named Ally. I basically moved in and house-sat for him. Every other weekend, and once or twice during the week, I'd go pick up Ryan and Brittany and bring them to Jody's house with me. They enjoyed it there; it had a pool and plenty of space. I lived there until September or October when Jody's season ended, then I got a place of my own.

Mysterious Ways

By that point, I'd gotten my Masters in Behavior Disorders at USF, but I could see the writing on the wall that the psychiatric hospitals which had been in vogue in the late eighties and nineties weren't long for this world. The insurance companies were driving them out of business. I was also, of course, in the middle of a divorce.

I got this tiny apartment right by USF, in a not so great neighborhood, but it was cheap and right near work. It was a one-bedroom apartment, with just one couch, a TV, and a bed. I had one of those little workout trampolines, the ones about three feet wide that you jump up and down on. That was Ryan and Brittany's bed when they came to stay with me. One day, I looked around and thought, *This is crazy. I can't provide for my kids. I gotta do something different.* I was making maybe $25,000 or $35,000 a year, I had two kids, and I was getting a divorce. I thought, *This ain't cuttin' it. What am I gonna do?*

That was about September or October of 1992. Everything had moved so fast—from getting the house, to getting divorced, to realizing I couldn't provide for my kids.

I had no plan, but the Lord works in mysterious ways. By January, I'd be leaving for law school.

How a Redneck with No Plan Got Into Law School

At the USF Psychiatry Center, two of my friends, Lois and Christine (Chris), started encouraging me to go to law school. I think I'd mentioned it maybe once, how I'd thought about it as a kid. And they were convinced I should do it.

I said no. I kept telling them, "Nah, I can't afford it. I've got kids."

They just kept pushing.

At some point, just to shut them up, I said, "Okay, fine. I'll get the little LSAT books and take the test, see how I do."

I took it, and it was brutal. I wasn't even *close* to passing.

Of course, that didn't deter them. They just said, "Well, you need to study."

So I studied, and took it again. Still awful.

At this point, my brother Jody was making millions (literally). So he told me, "Go take one of those Ka-plan courses. I'll pay for it."

I took the Kaplan course, and then I tried the test again. I did pretty well on the test the umpteenth time, and I was like, "Okay, but now what?"

I was still thinking I'd have to stay local. I mean, I was broke, and I had kids. There was only one law school in the area—Stetson. So I applied... and I got shot down.

Now, this was all happening very fast, all in the October to November time period of 1992. But by this point, I was thinking, *This is just not gonna happen.*

I had another friend, Nina, who I'd met through the Psychiatry Center. She worked for Hillsborough County as a teacher who would go teach students in their homes if they were homebound and couldn't attend school. USF had a

Me during a Christmas party at the USF Psychiatry Center

program where the homebound teachers would come into the Psychiatry Center, which is how I met her. There was also another homebound teacher who would come into the center, named Patty. We were all friends.

So, after I got rejected from Stetson, Nina asked, "Did you apply to South Texas College of Law?"

I laughed. "I've heard of Texas." But I'd certainly never heard of South Texas College of Law.

Nina said, "Well, apply."

Back then, applications weren't online. I had to fill the stuff out and mail it off. So I did it, and never heard back.

Maybe two or three weeks later, Nina came back—she didn't come to the center every day. I remember it was lunch time, in November of that year. She came in and asked, "Did you apply?"

I said, "Well, yeah, I sent my packet."

"Have you heard from them?"

"No," I said. And then I left for lunch.

My little apartment was right around the corner, so I walked home, ate lunch, and walked back.

When I came back in, Nina came over. "You're in," she said.

I shrugged. "Yeah, I'm in." I thought she was talking about getting back from lunch.

She stared at me and said, "No—you're accepted to South Texas. I called. You start in January."

I literally just started crying.

The Whirlwind

Nina had some money. Her kids had gone to South Texas College of Law, and she was a big donor. The rest is history, I guess—if you donate enough money, you can pick up the phone and make a call. That's how it works, God bless America, because that's what happened.

I didn't find this out until later, but South Texas College of Law was a frequent choice of law school for kids from Tampa. E.J. Salcines, a prominent legal figure and judge from Tampa, went there—so he started a pipeline that goes to this day from Tampa to

South Texas. If you look around the Tampa area, you'll find plenty of judges and lawyers who went to South Texas College of Law in Houston. I didn't know it at the time, but once you get to South Texas, it's like, "How come so many kids here are from Tampa?"

So after I stopped crying, I asked Nina, "What are you talking about?" There were all these thoughts running through my mind—I've got two kids. *How am I going to Texas? I'm broke. How am I paying for all this?* This was November, and she'd just told me I'm starting law school across the country in January.

From that point, things happened in a whirlwind.

Mom and Stinger put down the first $15,000 to pay for my first semester of law school.

That was just the first semester.

After that, I planned to take out loans—I ended up taking out about $60,000 to $70,000 in loans, which back then seemed like a *lot* of money. I was like, *I'm gonna have loans forever; I'm never gonna pay these off.* (But I did.)

I didn't want to leave Ryan and Brittany, but I figured out if I went to school year-round, instead of taking summers off, I could be finished in two and a half years. I planned to come home every month, or as often as I could, to see them. I told myself I could do that. Two and a half years... then I'd be back, and I'd actually be able to provide for my kids.

I had just rented that apartment near USF in September or October—by this time, I'd barely even been in it two months. So I stayed in that apartment until January, then I just slid my key up under the mat of the front office with a note: *I'm out.* I don't even know if they sued me for breaking my lease... I never heard from them again. I'm assuming they didn't, because I never got served papers in Texas. But that's how I broke my lease, with a little note: *Hey, I'm leaving for school. Here's your keys.*

I Hope You Fail

When I went to tell the kids goodbye, they were so little, they didn't even really understand what was happening. Brittany was only eighteen months, and Ryan was about five. I told them I had to go away to school. I don't remember it being traumatic for them, but for me, it was brutal.

I remember when I left, Kathy's last words to me were "I hope you fail!" Ouch. This became a motivating factor, like the words a coach puts on the walls in a locker room. "I hope you fail!" I was stunned. If I have Alzheimer's one day, I may not remember much, but I'll probably remember what she said to me.

I'm not trying to make her look bad—I'm sure she didn't understand why I felt like I had to go, or maybe she felt stuck herself and didn't know what to do about it, or maybe she was just still mad at me.

It was a blow, then, but eventually all was forgotten, kind of. I decided I would just have to prove her wrong... and I did.

God Bless Mom and Stinger

I mentioned that there were three people at the USF Psychiatry Center who worked there regularly: Lois (the supervisor), Chris (the elementary school teacher just a bit older than I was), and myself. A psychiatric hospital means a lot of stress, so we worked closely—we were all good friends.

The weekend I was leaving for Texas, I had a dinner to say goodbye to my friends on Saturday evening. I was supposed to go "home" to Mom and Stinger's that night to pack the car, and we were leaving Sunday. But after dinner, I wasn't quite ready to go home. So I stopped by Rance Harbor's, another buddy of mine, to hang out and say goodbye to him. And then I went back to Chris's (remember, there were no cell phones, so I just stopped by her house) to talk some more. We started having some beers—drank, laughed, cried, hugged, said our goodbyes. Nothing physical happened, we were just good friends. I was scared and needed reassurance.

I woke up with a brutal hangover Sunday morning—I'd fallen asleep on Chris's couch. I was like, "Oh man, I'm in trouble." I was supposed to have been home the night before to pack my car. I jumped up and rushed home. Did I say I was hungover?

God bless Mom and Stinger—they had all my stuff ready to go.

Everything I owned fit in two cars, Stinger's and mine. The three of us loaded up into the two cars that Sunday morning.

And off to Texas we went.

Part II

Off to Texas

———————————————————— PAUL REED

Chapter 4

This Thing Called Law School

Houston House

We drove straight out to Texas that Sunday morning. I'm sure we stopped at least once—I don't remember—but on Monday, we arrived in Texas.

South Texas College of Law was in downtown Houston, so Mom and Stinger put me up in a one-bedroom at the Houston House, one block from the college. It was a high rise building... I wouldn't even say it was an apartment building. It was more like an old hotel building that had turned its rooms into rentable suites. My hotel-room-turned-apartment had one room, then a closet that you walked through to get to the bathroom, and on the other side of that, a kitchen. It was a bit like the studio apartments you would expect to see in New York City or something—about 600 square feet. It only cost $500 a month, and that may have even included electricity. It was also a very convenient location, so a lot of South Texas College of Law students lived in that building.

Mom and Stinger helped me rent some furniture—a bed, a dresser, a computer (so I could type my papers for school), and a TV. There was just barely room to put everything. I put my clothes in the closet, and I used the top of the dresser as my desk.

The apartment couldn't have been any smaller, but it served its purpose, and I was thankful. I had a bed, and I was going to law school!

Later on Monday, or maybe on Tuesday, we checked out the school, and then Mom and Stinger said, "See ya later." I walked them down to the garage and came back up alone, then just sat down on my bed and started crying. I had never left home—even when I went to Manatee Junior College, I'd gone back to Brandon every weekend. Now, I was the farthest from home I'd ever been, and completely alone. I'd left my kids, I was still going through my divorce, and I was sitting in Houston in a high rise with nobody, not even sure how I was supposed to do this. There were no cell phones, and a call home was long distance; it wasn't like I could just pick up the phone and chat. I had no money; I don't even think I *had* a phone yet, because I still had to set up service. I was cut off from *everyone*, and starting law school in a matter of days. I was terrified.

I also had no idea that law school started the moment you walked in the door. We had arrived on the fourth or fifth of January, and classes were set to begin on the eleventh. Luckily, I walked over to the school at some point, and saw someone looking at a chart on the wall—a chart of *assignments*. Apparently, you were supposed to have your books and get started on your assignments right when you showed up. So I got my books, and started trying to read them and do my assignments. It might as well have been Greek, but I was expected to have them done before I attended the first class. So the next few days were spent preparing for this thing called law school.

The Paper Jesus Saved

At this particular point in time, at least for me, computers were all new. You hit F1 to save, and beyond that, I knew those function buttons all did something... but I didn't really know how to use them. There wasn't online stuff, back then. AOL was still in its infancy. So the only use for a computer was when you were typing a paper.

In law school, we were required to take Legal Research & Writing 1, and Legal Research & Writing 2. It was my first semester of law school, and I had to write a forty-page brief which included specific citations. You'd have to cite, for example, "Florida Second Appellate Court, on this date," etc. So writing this paper really was a process; it wasn't a paper you could write in one day.

I started working on the paper on Saturday or Sunday morning, and I'd been writing for about eight hours. I didn't know anything about saving or printing. I was just typing, looking at my books trying to get stuff right, typing, and typing some more... and the phone rang.

I answered, and it was Ryan and Brittany. I talked to them for a while, and when I went to hang up the phone, my arm brushed the on/off button of the computer. I looked back, and the computer was restarting.

I freaked out. The computer restarted, and when it booted back up, my paper was *gone*. I sat dumbfounded for a few moments, about to jump out the twenty-fourth floor window, no clue what to do. Then I thought about my buddy, Rance Harbor, who was a psychologist at the USF Psychiatry Center. He was a computer guy. So I called him up in a panic: "I don't know what to do!"

Rance was like, "Okay, okay, let me see what I can do to help," and he started walking me through places on the computer to look. We looked everywhere for that file, and there was nothing. It felt like forever, but it was probably about thirty minutes of Rance saying, "Try this, do this, reboot this," etc... and the file just wasn't there. Finally, Rance was like, "Man, I'm sorry; there's nothing else we can do."

I hung up that phone, and I was ready to pack up my stuff and go home. It was my first semester of law school, and this was a major paper. I'd already spent eight hours on it, and I didn't have time to redo it... I was just overwhelmed.

I decided to go for a walk to calm down. Houston House had this little convenience grocery store where you could get hamburgers, hot dogs, drinks, fruits and vegetables, etc. In southwest Texas, you could even get the big forty-ounce beers. So I grabbed this huge beer, and went outside. It was February or March, and it was freezing outside. I was just walking around town on Sunday, probably about dusk, with my giant beer, thinking, "What do I do? I can't believe this happened! I spent all day..." To be honest, I was close to considering just jumping off the balcony. Instead, I went back inside, and prayed, "Please, Lord," and booted up the computer.

I went back to where Rance said to look—where we'd looked a dozen times already—and there was this file just sitting there, named "Paul." I thought, *That wasn't there before.* But it had my name, so I clicked on it... and there was my paper!

To this day, I don't care what people say: God put my paper in that file, with my name on it. It was a freaking miracle. It felt like I'd been losing one minute before, and suddenly I'd won the Super Bowl.

From that point on, I was like *type, type, type—save—insert disk —save to disk—print.* By the time that paper was done, I had like seven thousand pages printed, one for every few lines I'd written, in case I had to take it to somebody to type up or something. But it all worked out.

I remember the paper being horrible—red ink everywhere from my professor—but that's neither here nor there. I had been *this close* to packing up and going home, and that disappearing/ reappearing paper was nothing short of a miracle.

Band of Brothers

I mentioned that in the Houston House, there were other law students from around the country.

One was Johnny Coburn, who lived a couple stories up. He was from Chicago, and we became best friends. To this day, we still visit each other.

Kendal Luke from Hawaii was another guy who became one of my best friends. He did not live in that building, but he came over often because it was a block from school—I still keep in contact with him, as well.

There was also John Simpson from Houston, Texas. John Simpson is the one I still hang around with the most. He was at my birthday party last July, and actually came into town just last weekend (at the time of writing this) to hang out at a rock concert Reed & Reed helped sponsor.

I made other close friends in law school, as well.

There was David Froneberger; he was married at the time, and he lived in Deer Park near Pasadena, about fifteen to twenty minutes away. His wife was a vice principal. I hung out with him a lot in law school, and I still do. He's now a judge.

Mike Scionti was a Tampa boy, but I met him in law school. He's still a great friend. He's a judge, too, and also a colonel in the military. When we left school, we all kind of lost touch with him, but apparently he joined the Judge Advocate General's Corps (JAG Corps). Later, I heard he was running for judge, and we rekindled a friendship after maybe twenty years. He was in Tampa, so I'm not sure why we lost touch for so long. Life happens.

There were other friends we hung out with, went to Mardis Gras with, etc., like Phil; we hung out with him regularly. But the six of us—Johnny, Kendal, John, David Froneberger, Scionti, and I— were together the most. They were my band of brothers.

Visiting the Kids

One of the biggest challenges of going to law school in Texas was one I knew I'd face from the start: I had to figure out how to do law school—studying, passing the classes and exams—and still be there for my kids. Ryan was five or six years old, and Brittany was about two. I had no money; I couldn't just fly home to see them. My car was one my Grandpa had given me, an old, four-door Dodge Diplomat, like the cop cars in the old TV shows. I was in law school about a month before I tried to make my first road trip home. This meant leaving on a Thursday, as soon as classes were done, and it was about a sixteen-hour drive. I drove all night. Pensacola was the halfway mark, and I reached there about three or four in the morning and pulled over at a rest stop—I had no money for a hotel. It was January, and cold, but I couldn't leave the car running with the heater because it would burn gas, and I couldn't afford the gas money... plus, you know, if I ran the heater with the windows up, I could die from the fumes. So I used a blanket, and I slept at the rest stop. As soon as the sun came up, I drove the rest of the way home. I got to Mom's about two or three in the afternoon, rested up a little, then around 5 p.m., I went to get the kids. I kept them Friday night and Saturday, dropped them back off Sunday, then drove straight through the entire sixteen hours back to Houston for an 8 a.m. class on Monday. When I drove away from my kids, I cried for hours. (As I write this book, it appears I cried a lot back then... This from a guy who never cried as a child.)

I made this trip regularly, the entire time I was in Texas, at least once a month and anytime we got off classes for a holiday. As I got further into law school and made friends, sometimes one of the guys would come with me. David Froneberger made the trip with me once, Mike Scionti would ride back with me sometimes since he was from Tampa, and one or two of the others... They were a good group of guys. If I had someone with me, we would take turns sleeping and drive straight through without stopping. About 10 percent of the time, someone would go with me, and the other times I'd go by myself.

One time, my buddy Kendal came with me. On the drive home, I tried my best not to blubber in front of him, to no success. But he understood. He said, "Don't worry about it. It'll be over before you know it." But that period of my life, driving off and leaving my kids behind... that was torture. I still get emotional when I think about it. Note: there was a lot of alcohol involved back then.

On a rare occasion, I would save up the money to fly. When I flew home, on those very rare occasions, I would ease the pain of leaving with a cocktail or ten. Back in the day, your buddies could meet you right when you got off the plane, rather than having to wait at the terminal. I remember on this one flight home after leaving my kids, I bought a bunch of tiny bottles of Crown Royal to drown my sorrows. My buddies told me later that when I walked off the plane, I was staggering, ping-ponging off the sides of the walkway ramp, dropping empty bottles from my pockets, then I saw them and yelled, "Hey, guys!" They still say that was one of the funniest things they'd ever seen. But that was my coping mechanism... when I flew back to Texas, I don't think I landed one bit sober, ever. Of course, if I was driving, I couldn't drink.

For two and a half years, that's what I did. I went to school in the summers, so there was no coming home for a month or two on a summer break. I just drove home every chance I could. I was in law school for eight semester terms: Spring, Summer, and Fall of '93 and '94, then Spring and Summer of '95... and that was it. I did law school in two and a half years instead of three. It meant giving up those two summers with the kids, but I saved six months that way. Otherwise, I'd have been in Texas through the end of the fall semester of 1995.

My Little Texas Girl

When I lived in Houston House, I had a friend we'll call "Yellow Lightning." She was attractive, with pretty blonde hair and blue eyes. She was the nicest person on the planet, and for a time, we were best friends. We didn't date, but there was definitely a physical attraction. I remember coming home often, and she'd be sitting outside my door, waiting for me. She was never upset that I'd been out without her, or that she'd waited a long time; she was just there, happy to see me.

Yellow Lightning was a sweetheart, genuinely the nicest human being I've ever met. She never said anything mean about anybody. We would hang out with friends or alone. If we happened to be in the same place, we'd go do things, and come back, but there was never an expectation to call one another, or to get together. Yellow Lightning was a true Texan. She got engaged right before I left Texas, and I remember her coming over once, just to visit me one more time since I might never see her again.

Texas girls, the ones I met, were just different—all very nice and down to earth—but my relationship with Yellow Lightning was special. She and I definitely cared about each other, but we never said *I love you*, and it never turned into anything deeper. I'm not sure why, to be honest; I never really thought much about why it didn't.

Yellow Lightning may have been the love of my life that never was.

Years later, she called me because somebody she knew had gotten in an accident here in Florida, and I lit up when I realized who was on the phone: "Oh, hey! How are you doing?"

I can say this now, I loved her!

Keith Interlude #4: The $5 Bet

This one happened while I was still in law school, and even though I wasn't there to see it, I sure heard about it later!

Keith went out to the USF area to a rock 'n' roll bar—heavy metal kind of folks. Keith was the kind of guy that could fit in anywhere, and then nowhere at all. Alcohol and "medications" dictated how the evening would go.

My buddies, Liston and Tony, just happened to be there when Keith and whomever he was with rolled in. They were the ones who told me this story, after the fact.

So, Keith was playing pool, and he won a $5 bet. I would not call Moreeder a pool shark, but he had his moments... like everything he did in life.

The guy who lost the bet didn't want to pay up. Big mistake!

Well, in Keith's mind, and mine too (you can ask my kids) when you make a bet, you pay up.

Keith and the guy got into a pushing match, but it got broken up. (Liston and Tony weren't involved, they were just watching.)

The guy left, but Keith just couldn't let it go. So they saw Keith chug his beer and get up—they said his eyes were like a shark, a predator stalking prey.

Liston and Tony followed.

Evidently, the guy was parked in the parking lot—it wasn't a big lot—and Keith was at the exit, standing there. Liston and Tony were at the doorway, watching.

The guy's car started coming toward the exit, and Keith started walking toward the car, then running. He jumped onto the guy's hood, smashed into the guy's windshield, and caved it in. The guy stopped as Keith rolled off the car. The guy should have just run over Keith and gone home, but who knew what was about to happen next? I guarantee you Liston and Tony didn't.

The guy started cranking up his window (this was before electric windows), and Keith was trying to hold it down.

The guy got the window up, but Keith had these alligator hands, just really tough—he punched the window, shattering it, and pulled the guy out: "You owe me five dollars!"

The guy gave Keith his $5.

Then Keith went back into the bar; his beer was getting warm. Gotta love Moreeder.

Keith told me about this before, but with Keith, you never knew what to believe. So it was several months later when I just happened to see Liston or Tony somewhere while visiting back home, I don't remember which one, and they said, "Dude! You're not gonna believe what your brother did!"

They told me the story, and I was like, *Holy cow! Keith was telling the truth on that one!*

I believe he broke his hand, and he went to Mom's house, and Mom said, "You need a cast. I can't put a cast on you. You need to go to the hospital."

Any time Keith messed himself up, he went to Mom. Poor Mom. Half the time, Mom would patch him up, unless it was too bad—but this time, Keith had to go to the hospital.

The guy didn't come after Keith for damages... back then, you didn't call the cops for things like that. You just fought things out, and you won or you lost. Besides, the guy might've realized he'd had it coming. I think there are country songs that say the same thing.

Buttmunch and the House in Pasadena

About six months into my time in Texas, Johnny Coburn and I found a house for rent in Pasadena. Pasadena was a small town—a dry town; they didn't sell alcohol. We got a house for $500 a month, and the drive to Houston was only about thirty minutes. Johnny took care of renting it, so I never actually met the owners.

It was an old house, with a large backyard. We had one of those little Smokey Joe grills that sit on the ground, and we'd get chicken or hamburger and cook out on that grill all the time. As I said, Pasadena was a *dry* town, but this house was right on the line, so our side of the street was a dry area, but on the other side of the street there was a Food Lion where we could get beer. You had to go to a liquor store to get the strong stuff. So we'd sit out there by the grill and drink beers, vodka, whisky...

Now, I've divorced liquor, but back then, I kept Crown Royal in the freezer. Johnny liked vodka. I did not know this until law school, but liquor does not freeze. Who would have thunk it?

When I mowed our yard, I would mow the yard for one of our neighbors, too, and in return he would keep an eye on the house if Johnny and I were gone for the holidays or a long weekend.

There was a kid who lived next door to the house, who'd come outside sometimes. He was little and cute, with blonde hair and blue eyes. Well, one day, that kid came out when we were sitting inside with the front door open, and he just flung a kitten into our living room and ran away.

We were like, "Holy crap! What are you doing?!" But the kid had run off, so we just kept the kitten. *Beavis and Butthead* had just started on TV, so we named the cat Buttmunch. Usually, we just called her Munch or Muncher.

She was a black, female cat, and I guess we unofficially adopted her. We didn't have a litterbox for her, we just left the bathroom window open—it had one of those window locks you could use to keep it up without it opening all the way—and she went in and out.

Johnny and I bought pump BB guns—looking back, I am really not sure why—and behind our house there were some electric wires, and then another house. Doves would come and sit on the wires, and Munch *loved* to eat doves. Johnny and I accidentally trained Munch as a sort of retriever: Johnny or I would pop one of the doves with the BB gun through the open window, and whenever we shot one, Munch would go get the dove, bring it to the window where she came in and out, and eat it. I mean, she ate the whole thing... there would be nothing left but wings, feet, and a beak.

If we shot one and it didn't fall on our side or it tried to fly away, she'd go chase it, get it, and climb the fence with the bird in her mouth to bring it back over. It got to where anytime we pulled out the BB gun, Munch would come running, jump the fence, climb up on the window sill, and wait. If we shot and missed, she'd fuss at us and look at us like, *You loser. You missed!* If we missed two or three times, she'd really freak out—she was ready to go. But I couldn't blame her; fresh dove probably beat that dry food we kept for her in the garage. One time, Johnny shot a dove, and instead of dropping, it flew onto the neighbor's house and then collapsed on their roof. We were like, "Oh

Muncher with a dove

crap!" We didn't want them to see a dead bird on their house. So we just chucked Munch up there and she grabbed the dead bird, jumped to a tree, and came back down with it.

If Johnny and I both went home for Christmas break or on a trip, we would just leave a twenty-pound bag of cat food sliced open in the garage with a kiddy swimming pool full of water for Munch, and when we came back, she'd be there. Once, Johnny and I flew back at the same time and when we both got back to the house, freaking Munch had like fifty cats in the garage! She'd thrown a party! We picked up the food, shut the window, and kept her inside for a few days. It took a while to get those cats to stop coming back.

Munch was an interesting little cat. When Johnny and I left Texas in the summer of 1995, Johnny took her with him to his girl-friend's house. Johnny called me a while later to update me. He said the first thing Munch did was jump up in the middle of Johnny's girlfriend's bed and take a dump. Munch had never been fond of Kelly when Kelly visited our house. Johnny was like, "Kelly is so mad!" Johnny and Kelly didn't last, and in the end, I'm not sure what happened to Muncher. But she was one heck of a cat.

Brittany One-Ear

I was coming home for Christmas break at the end of my second semester in law school, and since I didn't have any money, I tried to come up with a couple gifts for the kids that would show I'd put thought into them. I was going through some photographs and I came across this one of baby Brittany. She'd always had one ear that sort of stuck out, and I'd jokingly called her "Brittany One-Ear"... I thought it would be cool to make her a personalized t-shirt. So I went to a shop and had a shirt custom made that said *Merry Christmas*, with the picture under it, and then *Brittany One-Ear* under that. I brought it home for Christmas.

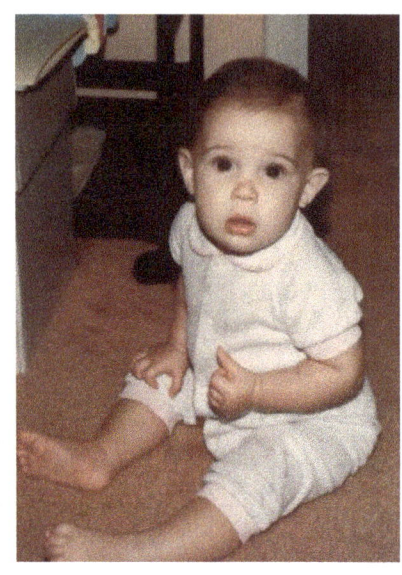

Brittany, as a baby

Brittany was about two years old at the time, so even though she didn't really appreciate the humor of the shirt, she wore it! But both Grandmother (my mom) and Mimi (Kathy's mom) *hated* it. To this day, I don't know which grandma got rid of it, but that shirt just disappeared and we never saw it again.

Lady Justice

A lot of my stories from law school begin with the phrase, "So we were at Hooters..."

There was a Hooters near campus, and we spent a lot of time there. In fact, we were there so much, the girls who worked there didn't believe we attended South Texas College of Law.

They said, "There's no way you're in law school with how often you're here!"

Kendal used to order these spicy crawfish there (yes, the Houston Hooters had crawfish), and he would literally just suck the eyeballs out of 'em. It was disgusting, but maybe that's normal in Hawaii?

Anyway, we were sitting there in Hooters one time, the usual band of brothers plus our friend Phil, and Phil was doodling on a napkin. I was talking to the girls, eating and drinking, and Phil held up this napkin to me and said, "You should get this as a tattoo."

The guys and me at Hooters in Texas. Left front: Mike Scionti. Left middle: Kendal. Left back: me. Right front: David Froneberger. Right middle: John Simpson. Right back: John Coburn.

It was just a sketch on a Hooters napkin, but it was Lady Justice, and she had STCL (South Texas College of Law) written on her blindfold, and she was holding the scales of justice. On the top scale, he'd written *Ethics*, and on the bottom scale were two green money bags.

I was like, "Oh, that's pretty cool!" It was certainly unique. Then I just stuck it in my jeans pocket and went on about life.

Around that time was when Johnny and I got our house in Pasadena. Now, in law school, once you get the feel of things, it's about two months of studying, working out, partying, whatever, like college... and then one month where you're in the library eighteen hours a day doing your work for tomorrow plus preparing for brutal exams. This was exam month.

One day, I was driving home from classes or an exam, and out of nowhere I reached in my jeans pocket and felt the napkin. I pulled the napkin out, and I was like, "Oh, I remember that."

Right about that time, I drove past a place and saw the sign: Southside Tattoos. I hit the brakes and turned around, thinking, *Let me just go see.* The tattoo parlor was everything you'd expect a place called Southside Tattoos to be. It was in a sketchy little strip mall, and as soon as I entered, a ZZ Top-looking guy came wandering out. He was a nice guy, so I pulled out the napkin. "A buddy of mine drew this up at Hooters. Think you could do this?"

"Yeah," he said. "Here, have a seat." He gave me a Coke and disappeared into the back, and about five minutes later, he came back out with a stencil. "You want it?"

I said, "Mom will kill me."

He shrugged. "Probably. But you want it or not?"

I asked how much.

"For you... fifty bucks."

I was like, "*Only fifty bucks?*" So I got it.

We all worked out back then, so it looked a heck of a lot better on my arm, in those days, than the slightly sagging version of it I have now.

Once I finished my exams, I came home for a visit on the next short break I had.

At the time, whenever I drove back home, I stayed with Mom and Stinger. They were living in the community next to Summerfield Golf Club.

So I was at Mom's, and I got a shower, then I came out into the kitchen with shorts on but no shirt, to get a drink. Their kitchen had cabinets with a gap underneath, which you could see through from the living room. I came out of my bedroom, into the kitchen, and I walked about halfway from the door to the kitchen, maybe four feet, before I heard Mom yell, "Freeze!"

"What?" I said, and kept walking.

Mom yelled, "Get your butt out here!"

I walked out into the living room, and Stinger said, "Oh, Junior, you're in trouble now!"

I got the full *What possessed you to do that?!?* talking-to. And that's how I introduced Mom to my tattoo.

It's a good thing she didn't know about all the *other* craziness I did in law school... that I'll get into in the next chapter. But since she's probably going to read this book, I guess she does now.

Chapter 5

Extracurricular Adventures

Mardis Gras

During that first year of law school, Kendal, Phil, Phil's girlfriend Kim, and I took a trip in the beater to New Orleans for Mardis Gras, the weekend before Fat Tuesday. ("The beater" was what they called my old car, because it didn't matter what happened to it; it could take a beating.) After classes on Friday, we drove the four or five hours from Texas to New Orleans. When we arrived Friday night, the only place with a vacancy was the airport Holiday Inn, about a half-hour drive from all the Mardis Gras activity. We checked into the hotel, and then drove down to the main drag where all the chaos was happening.

It seemed like there were a million people crammed into

The Beater

those New Orleans streets that Friday night. We pushed through the crowds and found a bar to go in and get a drink, then we just started making our way around the streets, checking things out. At some point, I had to use the bathroom, so we went into a bar. Now, all the bars were charging peo-

Part of our group in New Orleans

ple to use the facilities—you had to buy a drink or something—but there was a really long line to buy drinks, and I needed to go. The upstairs of the bar was closed, but I thought, *Maybe there's a bathroom up there.* I snuck upstairs to check.

It was dark upstairs. I looked around—no bathroom. But I was about to pee my pants. And remember, I had a buzz, to say the least. So I'm not saying it was the right thing to do, but I decided I'd just pee in the corner.

Next thing I knew, I got punched right in the side of the face, and while I was still reeling, a guy yelled at me, "You're going to jail!" with a choice name I won't repeat here.

I started fighting back. The guy and I were crashing around, knocking over tables. All the racket caught the attention of another guy who worked in the bar, and he ran up and jumped into the fight.

It was two against one, and all I could think was, *I'm not going to jail!* I was in law school. Even if the school let me stay, an arrest sure wouldn't look good when I applied to take the Florida bar.

The next part is kind of a fog, but later my buddies told me they were downstairs, wondering what was going on upstairs and where Paul had gone, when they saw me dive over one of the guys and tumble down the stairs—then I jumped up and ran out the front door of the bar, and I was gone.

However I got there, I was out on the street, shoving through the crowd, knocking people down in my panic to get away. I'd made it a few blocks, maybe, when a Good Samaritan took it upon himself to tackle me.

I thought it might be one of the guys from the bar trying to take me down, so I started fighting him.

A huge, black cop jumped in and broke us up.

By that time, one of my eyes was swollen shut, and my face was black and blue—I was a mess.

The Good Samaritan started rambling an explanation: "This guy was running, knocking people down, I was just trying to stop him!"

The cop said to him in a heavy Cajun accent, "You get out of here."

The guy ran off, then the cop turned to me. "Why you running? You okay?"

I explained to the cop what happened.

"They can't do that," he said. "You wanna press charges?"

I said, "To be honest, I don't even know which bar I was in."

The cop pointed at the street curb and said, "Just sit there, pull yourself together." Then he walked off to handle something else. So I sat. I didn't move an inch.

A while later, the cop came back. "You still here?"

I looked up at him. "You never said I could leave."

He shook his head. "Son, get out of here. Good luck to ya."

By this point, I was so lost, I wasn't even sure which direction I'd come from, much less how to find the bar where I'd left my friends. This was before cell phones, so I couldn't call any of them. I just headed down Bourbon Street or Canal Street, wandering aimlessly through the throngs of people.

It started raining.

I must really have looked a sight, then—one eye swollen shut, face bruised and swollen, dirty from the fight, and now sopping wet from walking through the rain with no umbrella in the wee hours of the morning.

I passed a girl on the street.

"Looks like you're having a rough night," she said. Then she invited me to breakfast.

We went and ate breakfast in a little cafe, and we just talked and had a good time. Toward the end of breakfast, the sun came up.

"Crap," I said. "I gotta get home." I had no idea where I was, but I knew our room was at the Holiday Inn near the airport.

So the girl walked me out onto the street where the cab drivers hung out, and she helped me get a cab—then she kissed me goodbye. "Have a nice life!"

I never saw her again.

The hotel was maybe thirty-five minutes away. I was in the cab, watching the meter, when suddenly I realized, "Oh crap, I don't have money." I dug in my pockets, and I had maybe seven or eight bucks. I had just spent one very long night in New Orleans, so I wasn't thinking far enough ahead to realize I could just get money from the guys when I arrived at the hotel. I just knew I didn't have the cash to pay the cabby. So I said, "Hey, I only have eight bucks. Can you still take me?"

The driver pulled over right there on the side of the interstate. "No. Get out."

I got out on the edge of the interstate, and the cabby drove off. I jumped over the barricade and walked down this steep, grass hill—right into the projects. I didn't know it then, but it was the Ninth Ward, probably one of the most unsafe projects in America at the time, before Katrina.

At that point, it was early morning and foggy, I had no clue where I was, and there were no phones to call anyone, so I just wandered through the fog to the bottom of the hill, where I saw a guy and a girl sitting out in front of their little duplex, smoking.

You can imagine how they stared at me—some white dude, eye shut, filthy, beat up, wet and muddy, just wandering out of the fog. They were like, "What the heck is *that*?"

I told them my tale, and long story short, they got me on a bus, then passed me from person to person at each bus stop.

About the second or third bus I got on, the bus driver was this big black man, with a thick New Orleans accent. By that time, I was looking like death warmed over. The bus driver took one look at me and said, "Boyyy, when I woke up this morning, if someone told me there was a white boy looking like you gettin' on this bus, I'd have bet everything I had that it wasn't going to happen!" Then he asked, "What brings you to bus number X" (I don't remember the bus number). I told him the story, and he laughed. "Yaa, that's why I don't do them Mardis Gras things anymore. It's crazy white boys like you who are makin' it so we good folks can't go down there anymore!" By this time, the whole bus was laughing. Then he said, "Come on, we'll get you where you need to be."

Eventually, the chain of people passed me to a non-English speaking, Hispanic woman who worked at the Holiday Inn as a maid, and they told me, "Just stay with her."

I stayed with her, and made it back to the hotel.

No sooner did I take a shower, get into my little red shorts and t-shirt, and crash into the bed, then my friends came barging in: "Where have you been?! It's time to go!"

So that was Friday... and I had to get up and do it all over again for Saturday.

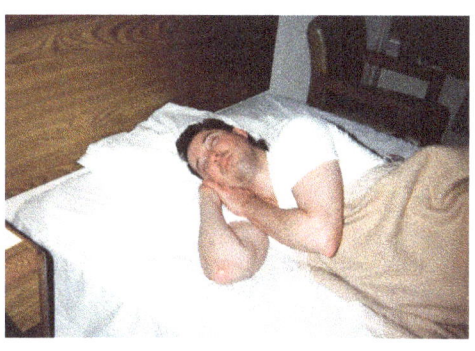

Me, sleeping soundly in the hotel in New Orleans... a picture my friends took right before they woke me up again.

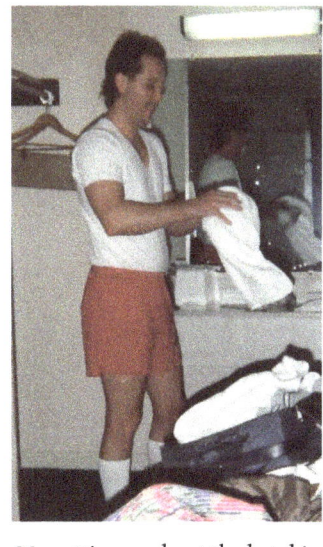

Me getting ready at the hotel in New Orleans

On Saturday, we stopped at a liquor store on the drive back to Mardis Gras, and bought these drinks that were basically like Hawaiian Punch with six shots of liquor in them. I have no idea what my friends did Friday night, but apparently it involved a lot of alcohol, because Kendal was drunk even *before* the Hawaiian Punch drinks. We parked on the side of the street in downtown New Orleans, and walked down the sidewalk. Kendal was staggering around for a while, then he passed out. So we just picked him up, threw him on the hood of the car, and let him sleep.

He slept a while, then we all went to get something to eat.

Mardis Gras was a crazy time. Just walking down the sidewalk, we saw a woman with a hypodermic needle hanging out of her arm, and there were women hanging out of balconies half-dressed, and people throwing beads

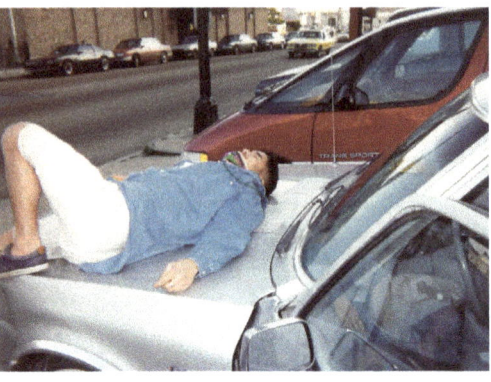

Kendal asleep on the hood of my car

everywhere. We were like, "What the heck *is* this place?!" That weekend, we even saw Chuck Norris fall off a float in the parade. He fell maybe ten feet off the float, then just got up and climbed back on. We were like, "Dude! Walker Texas Ranger just fell off the boat!"

Me, later that weekend, still beat up from Friday night

Saturday night, we left New Orleans to drive to Mississippi because Kendal wanted to do some gambling. I was wearing so many bead necklaces that my neck swelled up and I couldn't breathe. The guys had to get scissors and cut the necklaces off. When we got to Mississippi, they all went in and gambled, but I just stayed in the car.

Sunday morning was a silent drive home, almost like a drive of shame. However long it was from Mississippi back to Texas, no one said a word. We were spent.

We arrived in Houston on Sunday evening, exhausted... and then we all had to stagger out of bed bright and early for classes on Monday.

Never Disrespect a Matador

In late '93 or early '94, on a quick break from classes, Johnny and I took a trip down to Cozumel. We were just doing all the tourist stuff: we bungee jumped, rented a boat to go out and see one of the largest reefs in the world, and snorkeled off the pier. I bought a silver bracelet from some kid off the beach. While we were snorkeling, our Mexican guide tapped me on the shoulder and said, "Go down and look over there." I went back under, and there was a six-foot barracuda eyeing my shiny bracelet—he thought it was a fish, and he was about to eat me. *Woop*—I was up on that boat so fast! Paul was done snorkeling.

One of the things they had on the pamphlet for Cozumel was *Go see a bull fight*. I was like, "Well, I've never seen a bull fight, and I'll do anything once." So we went. We were out there in a big, concrete arena, and it was about 110 degrees outside.

The show started off with dancers—men with women in long dresses—then a horse show, and then a chicken fight. The chicken fight was brutal; the chickens literally killed each other. The final act was the bull fight.

Me, in the bullfighting arena, shaking hands with a random kid who came over to talk to us.

The matador came out in his full outfit, fancy green trousers and a green waistcoat with elaborate black embroidery, a black hat, and a little red blanket. He started getting the bull riled up. Then these men with spears came out and jabbed the bull right in the back, and the bull started bleeding down his sides. (I realize this is an animal rights horror story, and I believe many of these bull fights have been shut down since then. But I'm just reporting what we saw there.)

So now the bull was a bloody mess, and he was getting really upset at that matador. He charged the matador, who had gotten too close to the wall—he really got himself into a pickle—and the bull was attacking him.

Johnny started screaming, "Get him! Get him, bull!"

Suddenly, every person in that arena was staring at dumb and dumber—me and Johnny.

The men ran out and got the bull off the matador.

The matador got up, grabbed his little blanket, and put his hat back on, then walked over to the side of the ring and grabbed a big sword.

The bull, by then, was in the middle of the ring, out of breath and bleeding, not bothering anyone.

The matador looked right up at Johnny and me, and pointed the sword at us.

The people all stared at us, and I was like, "Johnny...We're gonna die. We disrespected the matador!"

The matador went over and jammed the sword right into the bull's throat.

The bull dropped, and while Johnny and I were still staring in shock, the matador strode back toward us, stopped maybe twenty feet away, and hurled the sword in our direction.

Before the matador got cornered

I hauled butt out of that theater. I was like, "Johnny, you can stay, do whatever you want, but I'm not gonna die here!"

I don't know if they still do those bull fights or not, and I'm glad I saw it... but it was one of those things I do not need to see twice.

New Suits

Johnny Coburn was from Chicago, and his grandmother still lived there. She worked at a Nordstrom or something, a high-end clothing store. Johnny needed to go back home for a wedding, and his grandmother offered to get us both the "Chicago discount" on some business suits if I came along. There was some sale they had running where her employee discount could get each of us three suits for the price of one. It was worth going to Chicago to get these suits, even with the cost of the plane flight (plane tickets didn't cost as much then as they do now), plus I'd never seen Chicago. I was like, "Yeah, I'll spend a couple hundred dollars and get some new suits!" Back then, a couple hundred dollars was a *whole lot* of money for me—not that it isn't a lot of money now, too—but nice suits were expensive, and this was a steal. So we both flew up there on a Friday.

Where we were staying at his grandma's was probably thirty to forty-five minutes from the city. It was November of 1993, and it was really cold in Chicago. Saturday morning, we drove into the city. We got our suits, and then Johnny dropped me off downtown. The plan was for me to do some sightseeing while he attended the wedding festivities. I only had on jeans, a shirt, and a leather jacket—no hat, no gloves—but when he dropped me off in the daytime, it was sunny and I was fine. I wasn't really thinking about how the evening would go.

I had a good time, and I went to all the sights: Sears Tower, a rock 'n' roll McDonalds, Soldier's Field, just all the tourist things, either walking or taking a taxi. (There were no Ubers back then.) Nike had a big store in Chicago, and at the time, Jody was still playing baseball for the Red Sox and had a contract with Nike. So I went in, spent an hour in the store, and picked out some shoes—I just gave them Jody's account number, and the shoes were free. (Having a brother in the major leagues definitely had perks.) All in all, I was just killing time, sightseeing. But eventually, I'd seen all I cared to see, and I was done.

It was evening by that point, and it was getting kind of cold and cloudy outside. Again, all I had on was jeans, a t-shirt, and a leather jacket. So I thought, "Eh, I'll go back to Johnny's grandma's house."

The plan had been for me to get to a train whenever I was ready, and ride the thirty or forty-five minutes to where his grandma lived. I got picked up by a taxi somewhere in Chicago, and I was heading back toward the train station when I looked to the left and saw a Hooters. I collect shot glasses and hot sauces, like souvenirs. So I was like, "I've got nothing to do; I'll go grab a beer and pick up a shot glass to take home." I had the taxi drop me off at Hooters.

I went in and sat down at the bar, and there was a guy there who looked to be in his forties. Now, I'm kind of a Chatty Cathy, so I struck up a conversation.

The guy was telling me what he did for work, when these two girls came in that were more my age, and the guy was like, "Oh, hey!" like he knew them, which he did.

The girls came over, and got to talking with me. Then one of the girls said, "Hey, you wanna go out with us?"

I had a buzz by this point, so I was like, "Yeah, sure!" Johnny was at a wedding, so I figured, why not? I'd go have some fun.

We went someplace, and we were talking and drinking. Around 7 p.m., one of the girls mentioned they had tickets to a Donny & Marie concert that was about to start. "You wanna go with us?" she asked.

Florida State was playing Miami that night, the game started at 7 p.m., and there was a Hard Rock nearby. So I was like, "Uh... no. Why don't you just drop me at the Hard Rock? I'll watch the game, and when you're done with the concert, you can come back and get me." So they dropped me off, and I found a seat at the bar.

Now, remember, I'm divorced from liquor *now*, but at the time... Well, when they came back for me at 11p.m., I was trashed.

But the girls weren't deterred. They asked me, "You wanna go dancing?"

Let me just pause this story to say that meanwhile, Johnny had gotten back from the wedding, and Paul was nowhere to be found. His family was all in a bit of a panic: "Where's the redneck from Brandon?" Johnny isn't like me; he worries about things. All he knew was he had dropped me in Chicago, it was almost midnight, we had to be on the plane at like seven or eight in the morning, and they hadn't heard from me. So they were calling the police, checking hospitals, thinking Paulie got himself killed or arrested or who knows what. So just picture all that chaos happening at grandma's, while I'm there hangin' with the girls.

The girls and I went from the Hard Rock to a bar that used to be a church building—you can't make this stuff up. It was a pretty cool place, and we were just dancing, having a good time.

Suddenly I looked down at my watch and realized it was like 3 or 4 a.m. It was *late*! At this point, the story gets fuzzy. I know I walked out; I don't remember even saying goodbye to them, but I may have.

So now I was outside in downtown Chicago at three or four in the morning. It was frigid outside, and all I had was that leather jacket. I was freezing to death. I was walking down the sidewalk, and I came across an exhaust vent from one of the skyscrapers. It was warm, so I was like, "Ahhhhhh," and I sat down right on the sidewalk in the dark, and fell asleep.

I don't know how long I was asleep, but it was still dark when a cop woke me up, asking, "Hey buddy, you okay?"

I told him what was going on, and he said, "You gotta get up, you gotta go."

I got up, and I knew I was supposed to be back at Johnny's grandma's, but I was hammered. So I stumbled into a nearby Marriot—I remember there was a guy buffing the carpets—and I just laid down on the couch in the lobby. I was toast.

Again, I don't know how long I was there—a minute, five minutes, an hour—but some guy came up. "Mister, do you have a room here?"

I was like, "No."

"Well," he said, "you can't stay."

At this point, I remembered Johnny had written down his grandma's number in case I needed him. So the Marriot guy let me use the phone, and I called.

Johnny was pissed. *"Where are you?!"*

Johnny told me the rest of this later, because I don't really remember any of this, but he said I told him, "I'm at the Marriot."

"You idiot!" he yelled. "There are ten Marriots in Chicago and we have to be on the plane in three hours!"

So I said, "I dunno, it's the one by the river."

"Great, you idiot, you've narrowed it down to five! Let me talk to the hotel guy."

So I gave the phone to the hotel guy, and evidently he explained to Johnny where I was.

Next thing I knew, the sun was up. I was sitting on the couch—the hotel guy let me stay because he knew Johnny was coming to get me—and Johnny stormed in.

"Don't say a freaking word," he said. "We're gonna get on the plane, you're gonna pass out, I'm gonna be pissed the whole time, then we're gonna get home and you're gonna go to bed."

I was just like, "Yeah man, okay."

So we got on the plane. Evidently, there was a stop in St. Louis (thank goodness no change of planes, because I don't even remember the stop), then the flight to Houston. So we landed in Houston, and I woke up.

"Man!" I said. "We're just now in St. Louis?!"

"You *%$#@!%^&!" Johnny said. "We're home!"

We got home, and I went to bed.

When I woke up later, Johnny said, "Shut up. I'm gonna be mad at you for a while."

I just nodded. "I'm sorry, man."

To this day, when we get together and reminisce, Johnny talks about this story like it happened yesterday.

So that's the Chicago story... but I did get my suits. Those three suits were the only nice suits I owned for years, even up through my first few jobs as a lawyer. (Thanks, Johnny's grandma!)

Why I Divorced Liquor

Scionti, Kendal, David Froneberger, and I went out to a bar one night during law school. Kendal, Scionti, and I were drinking, and David Froneberger was our ride. I'm not sure what all happened—to be honest, I barely remember the night. (This is why I don't drink liquor anymore.) Anyway, around three or four in the morning, the bartender told us, "We're closing. You gotta go." Evidently, it was time to leave. They kicked us out.

Scionti and Froneberger were gone—we couldn't find them.

So Kendal and I just started walking.

Eventually, we came to this huge intersection at Richmond. Just for scale, when the Houston Rockets won the world championship, there were like half a million people packed into this street; it's a main thoroughfare. And at that intersection was a Shell gas station, with a payphone over to the side of the parking lot.

We walked up, put our quarter in the payphone, and called John Simpson's house. He and Anne (who's now his wife) were at home. So John said, "Okay, stay there. I'll come get you."

The payphone was in the parking lot, the store was over to one side of us, and the gas pumps were to the other side. We sat down near the payphone to wait.

A few minutes later, a car full of some kind of gangbangers pulled up and parked about fifteen feet from us, blasting Mexican music, trying to be all tough looking. Several guys and some women climbed out of the car.

One of the women was pretty hot. Kendal was staring—maybe he said something to her, I'm not sure—but suddenly one of the Mexicans dove at Kendal, and next thing I knew, we were in a brawl with the Mexican guys.

Now, remember, this wasn't an isolated gas station; it was a major intersection, and now we had an at-least-six-person brawl going down in the parking lot.

I remember looking over at some point, and Simpson's beat-up S-10 pickup truck was waiting there at the light, in a left-turn lane. Well, he must've spotted the fight, because suddenly he blasted over the curb and across traffic—he wanted to get in on the thing!

By this point, there were a lot of people fighting us. We were outnumbered.

Simpson swung into the parking lot and jumped into the fight, and then sirens started blaring in the distance.

I was like, "Dude! We gotta go!" I was thinking everyone would run to Simpson's truck, so I broke free, ran to the truck, and jumped in. There was Anne, staring at me. "What are you doing here?" I asked. "Where is everyone?"

Anne said, "They're still outside!"

So I got out of the truck and ran back into the fray.

About the time I jumped out, Kendal was taking a guy right over the bushes. I didn't see Johnny. The next thing I knew, the cops flooded in from every direction, slamming us against whatever surfaces they could find. They pulled Kendal, John, and me over to one side of the parking lot, and the Mexicans over to the other.

I got slammed up against the payphone, and the cop said, "You got ID?"

I said, "Yeah, yeah, in my wallet."

"I'll get it," the cop said. He pulled my wallet out, and there next to my driver's license was my law school ID. The cop cursed, then said, "Wait here. Don't move."

If you get arrested while in law school, you aren't automatically kicked out—*automatic* would be too strong a word—but it definitely crossed my mind that we were done.

He went away, and a few moments later, the cops were shouting, "Okay, everybody, get out of here!" Evidently, they were familiar with the law school, and didn't want to arrest us.

As we walked toward John's truck to leave, Kendal tried to charge one of the Mexicans! (We called him Kendal the Red, because when he got mad, he just saw red, like a bull.)

So I tackled Kendal. I grabbed him by the head, dragged him into the bed of John's truck, and yelled, "We gotta go!"

Everybody piled in, and John peeled off—we were outta there!

I counted us lucky to get out of that one the way we did... but nights like that are why I divorced liquor.

One Heck of a Night

One night, the guys and I got tickets for a rodeo. We invited three or four of the girls we were friends with. Another friend was also joining us, a pompous guy we called Olympics because he had been to Olympic tryouts for swimming, and he was always bragging about it. He had money, and he wore all these expensive clothes and fancy shoes.

Anyway, it was winter—cold and icy outside—and our group was walking up toward the rodeo when one of the girls just ran up and tried to jump on my shoulders. I wasn't prepared, and I slipped on the ice. *Bam*, down we went! I dislocated my shoulder, and the girl face-planted. She was bleeding all over the place. We never made it to the rodeo. The girl left, and I probably should've gone to the hospital—I was in a lot of pain—but I didn't. And then out of nowhere, Olympics headed off with some girl and left us.

The rest of us went back to Kendal's apartment. I put ice on my shoulder, and we drank. Around four or five in the morning, Kendal got hungry and made a big pot of rice. One of the other guys was already hungover and vomiting. (We used to drink like that a lot, but alcohol is a harsh companion!)

Right about then, there was a knock on Kendal's door. We opened the door.

Olympics was standing there, one shoe missing, shirt and slacks all dirty, one leg covered in mud, ghost-pale, and shivering. Apparently, he'd gone somewhere with that girl, they'd gotten into an argument, and she threw him out of the car into the mud on the side of the road. He'd lost one of his fancy Bruno Magli shoes in the mud, and then walked all night in the cold *with one shoe* to get back to Kendal's house.

Just then, one of the girls that lived in Kendal's apartment came downstairs. I think she was going for an early morning run. She stopped and stared at us—Olympics pale and freezing at the front door, the other guy outside in his boxers throwing up in the grass, me lying on the floor with a bag of ice on my shoulder, and Kendal standing at the stove in the kitchen eating rice straight out of the pot with a spoon.

She said, "That had to be one heck of a night."

My band of brothers and I had many more adventures... not all of them made it into this book. It's a wonder we all survived, much less graduated from law school, to be honest—and not just because of the exams.

Chapter 6

Graduation and
Goodbyes

Graduation Party at the Cattle Ranch

John Simpson's family had a cattle ranch about two hours away from Houston. That final semester, when we all graduated, John hosted a graduation party at the ranch for our "band of brothers." John, Johnny, Kendal, David, Michael, and I were all there, plus all of our parents. The party was scheduled for a Saturday, but us guys—along with some of their girlfriends or wives—headed up on Friday to stay at the ranch for the weekend.

Anyway, the property was huge, like four hundred acres or so. At some point, Simpson said, "You want to see the haunted house?" What happened next was exactly like *The Blair Witch Project*, but without the cameras... Johnny, Kendal, John, and me, with some of the girlfriends/wives, all hiked a mile or two through woods in the middle of nowhere, back to this "haunted house."

We got there, and it was this ramshackle cabin in the woods. John said, "Be careful when you go in! There could be animals."

So I was thinking lions? Tigers? Bears? I didn't know what the heck they had in Texas.

It was pitch black inside the house, and John said, "It's haunted, so I don't know what's going to happen!" He kicked in the door, and everyone jumped.

Then a huge buzzard rushed at us from inside the house, squawking and flapping its wings! It seemed like ten feet tall!

We all screamed and ran, but when we realized it was just a bird, we all burst out laughing.

We started walking back the mile or two to the main house.

On the way back, suddenly there was this deafening noise, and a voice screaming, "You're gonna die!"

We all freaked out, hauling butt through that field, dodging piles of cow poo, pee running down our pants... and finally John yelled, "It's just my dad!"

He was laughing himself half to death—his dad had been lying in wait for us with a hand cannon. He scared the crap out of us!

So that was Friday night.

These rednecks living out in the middle of nowhere had to make up stuff to do for fun, and they were pretty creative. On Saturday, they brought out this old beat-up truck, an old Chevy or something. It was their work truck on the farm. The Simpsons had an irrigation system that they just moved around the farm with the truck, so they brought it out and soaked a big field. Then we spent the rest of the day getting dragged through the mud behind the truck by a rope, riding on a piece of cardboard like a sled. There was cow poop flying on everybody, and water everywhere. People were rolling off and wrecking, or trying to ride two or three at a time, fighting and pushing each other off—not your normal graduation from law school, but I swear, it was one of the funnest experiences I've had in my whole life.

When we finished doing that, we all got in the truck, and were driving back to wherever—it was a big, big ranch; we didn't know where we were going. John had these two bags, like burlap sacks or feed bags, in the back of the truck.

He stopped the truck in the middle of a field and said, "We're going to do something else now."

We were all like, "Okay. What?"

John said, "I'm gonna stay in the truck, and you guys get out and just start walking until I tell you to stop."

We got out, and we walked probably a hundred yards or so. We were about a football field's length away from the truck when John told us to stop.

He pulled out this big stick or a shovel or something, and started beating on the side of the truck.

We were all standing there, wondering what the heck he was doing, when suddenly the ground just started rumbling, and there was this thundering sound—

It was a stampede: a horde of longhorn cattle, coming right at us.

We started yelling, "Run!"

We sprinted back toward the truck, and the cattle were coming at us from every direction, all headed for the truck! Some of them were beating us to it, coming from the left or the right, but the big herd was behind us.

We reached the truck and dove in, and *boom!* The cattle were ramming the truck, rocking it back and forth.

John was like, "Oh, yeah, they like these treats." He opened up the bags he'd brought, and inside were these things that looked like little tater tots. For the next hour, we stood in the back of the truck, feeding the cows those treats. But that was insane!

After that, it was time for the party.

All the parents arrived... Kendal's family was from Hawaii, so his mom brought us all legit Hawaiian leis. It was awesome! Kendal's dad was there, too. He was a short guy, nice as heck, a lawyer in Hawaii. Mom and Stinger were there, and so was John's dad. John's family had kegs, and after a while, most of us were pretty hammered.

John's girlfriend (now wife) Anne was there—she wasn't much of a drinker. Also, John had graduated high school at like sixteen and went to law school at twenty-three or twenty-four, so they were both still pretty young. I remember someone whipped out the tequila. Anne drank a bit, then flat passed out. Somebody even took a picture of it. We still bust her $%&# about that night.

Now, Stinger, who pitched for the Red Sox in the '67 World Series, and the other old timers, they knew their ball. They knew their World Series guys. Kendal's dad was a gambler; he'd probably even bet on that game. So they'd gotten a bit drunk, and Kendal's dad just started ragging Stinger, saying, "I could've been an All Star if I hit against *you* every day."

Stinger came back with, "You wouldn't have lasted *one* day

with me, because I'd have put that &$!% ball right into your %$!&$!% ear and killed ya!"

Everybody was shocked, then we all just started laughing—but nobody ragged Stinger after that.

The meal we had at that party was the best meal I've ever had in my life. They had a giant, redneck grill—hundreds of pounds of meat on that grill cooking, and you could smell it a mile away. There was no processed meat; it all went straight from the field onto the grill, and it was unbelievable: the juiciest hamburgers you ever saw, the best steak you ever ate in your life, barbecue beef like no other, baked potatoes the size of watermelons, and corn on the cob. We all sat down with Dixie paper plates and mason jars for our drinks. It was exactly the kind of feast you'd expect Paul Reed the redneck to eat at his graduation, and I've never had a meal that good, before or since.

Our graduation party was a little different than going to the Ritz, or whatever fancy thing people might usually picture for law school graduation—but it was perfect. If you ask me what I did for my USF graduation, I couldn't even tell you, but that graduation weekend from law school, at the ranch... *that*, I'll remember forever.

Ringing the Bell

At South Texas College of Law, they had a giant bell, and whenever you finished your final exam of law school, you rang the bell one time. The tradition was that however many times you rang the bell was the number of times it would take you to pass the bar. Well, I'm not superstitious. I rang that bell a bunch of times. I was done with law school!

Last Night in Pasadena

When everything wrapped up with law school and graduation, Johnny and I went back to pack up the house in Pasadena.

We had a whole house full of stuff—couch, futon, computers, beds, this, that, and the other—but we could each only take whatever fit in our cars, so we had a garage sale out front on one of the days beforehand, selling stuff.

The night before we were both planning to leave, the guys came over. We were all heading our respective ways the next day, and we didn't know if we'd ever see each other again. Oh, we had every intention of doing so—we were close—but you just never know. We had a pretty decent backyard, so we started a little fire, and we were all just hanging out, drinking, telling stories, saying goodbye or whatever.

Well, John Coburn was a pyromaniac.

Next thing I knew, he hauled the futon out of the house—the futon had a wood frame—and threw it on the fire.

We thought it was hilarious, so then the guys started throwing more and more stuff from the house into the fire—furniture, clothes, computers, whatever they could find that wouldn't fit in Johnny's car or my car to take home.

At one point, Kendal grabbed a saw and went over to the edge of the neighbor's yard, and he started sawing down trees to throw in. We were like, "Kendal! You can't cut down the trees! We're leaving!"

By now, the fire was *huge*. I mean, you'd have thought the house was on fire.

Then we heard a fire truck. Now, we were pretty buzzed, so we were like, "Hey! It sounds like it's getting closer!"

The fire truck pulled up into our yard, and we were like, "Oh crap! They're here for *us!*" We were laughing, like, "Hey! What's going on?"

The firefighter was not amused. He said, "What the heck are you guys doing?"

So we told him we had just graduated from law school, that Johnny was from Chicago and I was from Florida, and that tomorrow we were both going home...

CHAPTER
SIX

The firefighter was like, "Well, you can't burn down Pasadena, you idiots! Put the fire out!"

We were like, "Yes, sir. Yes, sir. We're sorry."

He asked, "Do you even have a hose?"

"Uh... no."

All of a sudden, his alerts went off, and he said, "We got another call. I gotta go. Idiots, put the fire out."

And they left. They'd gotten another call with a real emergency.

We just let the fire burn out.

Outside the house in Pasadena

Everybody woke up the next day, and that was it. I got in my old beater, packed with my clothes and not much else, and left law school.

That was the end of two and a half years in Texas—from January of 1993 until July of 1995.

I finally came home.

Part III

Back to Florida

Chapter 7

Becoming a Lawyer

Studying for the Florida Bar

For the first two years after I moved back from law school, I lived with Mom and Stinger down in Sun City Center, about thirty minutes south of Tampa.

The bar exam is only offered twice a year—in July and in February—and I'd missed the July bar. I wasn't ready for it, anyway, because while law school gives you the basics, it doesn't cover the specific state laws that you have to know for the bar exam, especially Florida law. Preparing for the bar was really like going to law school again, just from home this time. I bought study materials—a big stack of books four to five feet high—on Florida law. I had a computer disk with 2500 questions on it, and audio cassettes that went along with the books. I studied six days a week, Monday through Saturday. I took some Sundays off—I might play ball or something—but the rest of the week, I studied at least eight hours a day.

Some days, I'd leave Mom's house in Sun City Center and drive to the USF library to study. If I was at Mom's, I'd put in the computer disk and answer the practice questions. They each had five options—A, B, C, D, or E. The Florida bar is a beast, because A could be right, B could be right, C could be right... the question was which one was *most* right. I'd read each question, read the options, and do my best to answer. If I got it wrong, a little thing would pop up that would explain the correct answer and why. I was also working out back then, for stress, so other days I'd just go to the gym, and listen to the cassettes while I worked out.

I didn't take breaks from this routine, except for when I had Ryan and Brittany. I brought Ryan and Brittany to Mom's every other weekend, and sometimes I'd go down on a Tuesday or Wednesday and take them to McDonald's or something. When I had Ryan and Brittany for the weekend, I studied on the computer after they went to bed. Mom and Stinger's community had a swimming pool, and they lived on a golf course, so we'd hang out and do whatever—and then I'd take them back to Kathy's on Sunday.

I had zero money, but I didn't get a job, because Mom and Stinger—God bless them—said, "You gotta study. You gotta pass." They knew I didn't know Florida law yet; I hadn't gone to a Florida school. So they supported me.

Needless to say, when the time for the bar exam arrived in February, I was feeling pretty confident. The bar is a two-day-long ordeal: a three-hour essay in the morning, then a three-hour multiple choice test in the afternoon, for two days in a row. There were a bunch of others staying in the same hotel I'd chosen, who were also taking the bar. After the first day of the test, I saw a lot of them studying in their rooms, on their porches, trying to cram in that extra review time... but I went out to Hooters and had a beer and some wings. I'd studied; I was done. I figured there was nothing new I would learn between that night and the next day's test.

On the second day, people were walking into the test still holding their books. I finished the exam and left an hour early. I lived four hours away from where they held the test, so by the time the bar exam officially ended, I was already hauling butt on Alligator Alley, heading home. I knew I was probably the only one who handed in my test before they said *Time's up*, but I was confident.

A lot of people do fail; the Florida bar has a pass rate of about 60 percent, maybe. But I did really well—and the rest was history. (I guess it really doesn't matter how many times you ring that bell at South Texas—I only had to take the test once!)

Keith Interlude #5: Tire Kingdom

When Keith was younger, he had a series of jobs: he drove one of the safety vehicles that led the way in front of oversized trucks, he was a phone person for cable TV, and for a while he was even a car salesman—and that man could sell cars! At every job, he would work long enough to get some money, then he would either quit or get fired. One of his jobs, back in those days, was at Tire Kingdom.

Keith's job at Tire Kingdom in Brandon actually made the newspaper, and Keith got sued because of it. I don't remember if I was a lawyer yet, then—I just remember I said, "I'm not getting involved with this one."

Anyway, Keith was working at Tire Kingdom, and they happened to have some $40 for four tires deal running.

A guy came in, but the tires that were on sale were only for one specific type of car, and wouldn't fit his car. The guy got mad because the store wouldn't honor the sale for the type of tires he needed.

The manager was trying to explain it to the guy, but he was getting more and more upset.

Keith, being Keith, couldn't just let the manager handle it. He got into it with the customer, and it led to some kind of fight. Now, this guy was bigger than Keith. I don't remember for sure, but there may have been a crowbar involved. Keith panicked, and climbed up the tire racks on the wall, then started throwing tires down at the guy. Tires!

They were landing on top of the guy, hitting him in the head... it totally messed the guy up.

Anyway, Keith got sued, Tire Kingdom got sued, the manager got sued... Did I say it made the newspaper? I remember reading about it: "Guy Sues Tire Kingdom," or whatever the headline was. Tire Kingdom had lawyers, but Keith got sued individually, too. I think Tire Kingdom took care of it, and ended up paying the guy.

But that was Keith... He would jump in with the best of intentions, but he didn't know when to stop.

Trampoline Regrets

When Ryan was about eight or nine and Brittany was five, I surprised the kids with a trampoline—against Kathy's strong advice. (You can see this very trampoline pictured here.)

A week later, Brittany broke her middle finger.

Brittany was supposed to go skiing with

Assembling the Trampoline

Mimi and Poppy soon after that. She did, but her cast wasn't waterproof so they had to wrap it in a plastic bag.

I don't remember if anyone said "I told you so"—but they probably did.

Keith Interlude #6: Halloween Costumes

At one point, Keith was married to a woman named Gina. They were married for over ten years, but they had issues. After a while, I stopped going out with them altogether, because you just never knew what was about to go down when you were with them.

Anyway, after law school, while I was studying for the bar, I was dating this girl named Holly. She lived in some apartments on 301 and Bloomingdale. It was her birthday, so about eight of us went out to Bennigan's or Chili's, some place like that, to celebrate. The group included Holly and I, Keith and his wife Gina, plus a few other couples who were Holly's coworkers and friends.

Jody had just bought me a brand new Ford Escort. It was only a couple months old.

We went out, and then we all headed back to Holly's apartment. Gina must've been talking to one of the guys who was out with us at some point, and it rubbed Keith the wrong way. We weren't even out of the car yet, and Keith wanted to kill the guy.

I was like, "You've got to be kidding me; he didn't even do anything!"

But Keith was convinced the guy had been hitting on Gina.

I told Gina, "Keith's drunk. Take him home."

Gina said, "I'm not taking him home!" (This was just what they were like. Honestly, it was exhausting.)

By now, it was about 1 a.m., and Keith said, "Give me the keys to your car, or I'm gonna go beat the guy up."

I said, "You're drunk! I'm not giving you the keys to my new car!"

But Keith was going on and on, threatening to kick the crap out of the guy, and I knew he'd do it. So finally I said, "Screw you!" I threw the keys at him. "I hope you die!"

I'm not proud of it, but I said it.

Keith took my keys, and drove off.

I got the police report later... He hadn't even been in the car two minutes before he was doing seventy miles per hour on Bloomingdale. He tried to pass a tractor trailer, but there were oncoming cars. Rather than have a head-on collision, Keith tried to cut back in, and clipped the semi. It threw him back into the cars, and he smashed into them head-on. It was a bad accident. He got airlifted to the hospital.

We didn't even know about it until the next day.

Holly and I and the others had all stayed at her apartment— there were people sleeping on couches, on the floor, wherever. The next morning, I woke up to the phone ringing. This was back when we had answering machines. So then I heard Mom's voice on the answering machine: "Paul! Paul, are you there? Answer the phone! Your brother's in the hospital! He may die!"

I was like, "*What?!*"

I called her back, and she told me what happened.

Gina was asleep right there on the floor, and I shoved her awake with my foot. "Get up! Keith's in the hospital!"

Of course, he didn't die—but he was messed up. Punctured lung, broken this, broken that.

Keith got sued for the accident, and I got sued because it was my car he was driving.

Now, Keith had a drug charge already, and he was on proba-tion. So what does Bright-Eye think? *I'm leaving.* Apparently, his plan was to abscond to Tennessee. So in the middle of the night, he tried to pull the tube out that was inflating his punctured lung. Well, it was sutured in. He gave it a yank and caused himself excru-ciating pain, so he was screaming.

The nurses heard it and came rushing in.

He was like, "Get this out of me!"

They said, "Mr. Reed, you need it."

"Get it out!"

He was on the fifth or sixth floor, with a messed up lung and broken bones, but he detached from everything and he and Gina hobbled down the stairwell. Off to Tennessee he flew.

I was living with Mom and Stinger at the time, studying for the bar six to seven days a week, so I decided to move into Keith's house. (He was living in what had been Grandma and Grandpa Reed's house).

At some point, a year or more later, Keith and Gina decided to come back. Gina had relatives in Lake County, in the panhandle area of Florida—it's a little, one-judge county. They stopped there for a visit on their way back down, and evidently, they got into some kind of domestic beef while there, and Gina called the cops.

SWAT came out.

Keith knew he was in trouble—he had his previous charges, and now the DUI he'd fled from. They were knocking on the door, but he stayed on the bed smoking a cigarette. When they busted in, he just put his hands up and let them handcuff him.

Eventually, Keith went to court, and I represented him.

So we walked into this little podunk courthouse with no air conditioning, like we were in Mayberry or something. I looked around, wondering, *Where's the judge?*

The judge was in his office with a little window unit, holding court in the air conditioning. So we got called, and went back... and it was a nightmare. We had *no* chance. Gina testified, Keith testi-fied, I asked a couple questions —and the judge said, "Guilty." Keith got ninety days in the county jail.

Now, in these small counties, they get federal dollars for having prisoners. So nobody left the courthouse without doing some time in jail.

When it was time for Keith to get out, Halloween was approaching. So Keith, being Keith, thought it would be a great idea to get us a couple of costumes. He stole two jumpsuits as he was leaving the jail—the white and red county correctional institute jumpsuits with the hats and everything.

That's just how Keith was... not the brightest, but thoughtful in his own, strange kind of way.

I was like, "Dude—you go to jail, and what you think about when you're leaving is stealing from them?" You gotta love Moreeder!

I actually did wear mine for Halloween.

First Job as a Real-Life Lawyer

In law school, everybody takes the same courses—whether you go to Harvard, Stanford, Stetson, South Texas, or somewhere else.

There's Torts 1 & 2 (a "tortfeasor" is the negligent party in an injury case), Contracts 1 & 2 (for writing and understanding contracts), and Property 1 & 2. (These classes are a joke, because they talk about old England. If they're teaching the same stuff now that they were when I took it, half of it wasn't even applicable to today. Plus, it never covered what you'd actually need to understand about local property rights like title companies and imminent domain. Those were all things I had to learn after I got out of law school). They also make you take Civil Procedures (State Civil Procedure, and Federal Civil Procedure); Wills, Trusts, and Estates; some Legal Research and Writing classes; and a few electives.

When you graduate law school, you know a little bit—but it's all standard stuff, no specifics, and you're no more a lawyer when you pass the bar than a man on the moon would be. Technically, you are, but you're not *really*. You become an actual lawyer once you get a job and start practicing law.

So that's where I was.

The first job I got after I passed the bar was in 1996 down in

Fort Myers, a couple hours away from Brandon, at a personal injury firm. The owner's wife wasn't a lawyer like he was, but she worked as the office manager. I went down, interviewed with them both, and they liked me.

I told them at the interview, "Look, every other weekend, I gotta go home. I've got my kids."

They were okay with it, at first. So I rented a tiny, one bedroom apartment in Fort Myers, a month-to-month kind of thing, and I moved down there.

I didn't know anybody, so all I did was work from 7 a.m. to 8 or 9 p.m., go home and eat, go to bed, and do it all over again the next day. When I was there, I worked Saturdays. Every other Friday, I drove to Brandon and picked up the kids, then took them to my Mom's in Sun City Center for the weekend.

Several times, I was supposed to leave on Friday, but the owner or one of the others would say something had come up, and they needed me to work Saturday. I always said no. They were mad, but I still came home and picked up the kids.

After several weeks or so, that firm wanted me to sign a three-year contract to work for them. I drove home that weekend to pick up the kids, and I was thinking, "What do I do?" I was only seeing the kids every other weekend, rather than being able to stop in midweek to grab dinner, or go to their games and whatnot like I did when I lived closer. And all I did in Fort Myers was work, eat, and sleep. Basically, I was miserable... but it was a job.

Well, I don't even remember saying this, but apparently when I was going back and forth from Texas, I must've told the kids that once I came home, I'd never leave again. So I picked up Ryan and Brittany that Friday night, and one of them said to me, "Dad, you said when you came home, you wouldn't leave again!"

I went back to Fort Myers on Monday, and quit.

Keith Interlude #7: Keith's Daughter

At some point, when Keith was seventeen or eighteen, he got a girl pregnant. Keith was Keith, and the girl and her family wanted nothing to do with him, so they never told him. Keith didn't even know he had a child.

Then Facebook, the internet, and the like came about... So twenty years after the fact, Keith stumbled across something, and he said, "I think I have a daughter."

We hired a friend of ours who's a private investigator, Wally from our old neighborhood (believe it or not), to look into it. Lo and behold, Keith was right! He had a daughter.

Keith on his motorcycle in 2003, with his dog, Petey, behind him.

Keith tracked her down, and they reunited (or *united*, I should say, since they'd never known each other), and they became very close! She had children, and just like that, he was Grandpa Keith... He would go up to Barnesville, Georgia to visit them in his Corvette, flashing money, buying crap, like he was king of Barnesville. But he was ecstatic to unite with his daughter and grandkids. His daughter was a sweetheart. She is a teacher. To this day, they still go visit and vacation at Mom's when they can, in Melbourne Beach.

Cutting My Teeth

After I moved back to Mom's, I started applying for jobs again. These days, you apply online, but then, it was all paper applications. I applied at the state attorney's office, the public defender's office, everywhere I could.

Back then, Stetson College of Law in Tampa had reciprocity with South Texas College of Law, meaning South Texas students or graduates could use the Stetson library. The Stetson library had an employment bulletin board, with little three-by-five cards pinned up with different job listings. I'd go in and scan the board, find jobs I might qualify for, then write down the name, address, and phone number of the company.

Some cards said they wanted the "Top 10 Percent" graduates—I didn't even have to write those down. My job search got narrowed pretty quickly, because I was a newbie with basically zero experience. But then I saw a card for one firm that was looking for an entry level attorney, with zero to three years of experience. I was like, "Okay, I can do this one," so I called the number, and they scheduled me for an interview.

This firm had an office in Bradenton, and another right across the Skyway Bridge in St. Pete. The St. Pete office was where my interview was to be held. So I put on my suit the day of the interview, drove to St. Pete, and went into the office.

I was looking around while I waited, reading the things on the wall, and I noticed that the attorney I was there to interview with was from Milwaukee, where Jody had played baseball for a time.

So the attorney walked in, and he was only a year or two older than I was—I was thirty-one at the time, but I'd gone to law school late, so he'd already been working with the firm for a while. (As I learned later, he's a great attorney.) We shook hands.

I said, "You're from Milwaukee? My brother played for the Brewers."

We talked about baseball for over an hour. Not a peep about the law, or where I went to school—just guys talking ball.

At some point, we noticed it was dark outside, and he said, "Crap, I gotta get! I'm in trouble." (He was married, and his wife was probably waiting for him.) Then he looked at me and said, "You want a job?"

I was like, "Yeah!"

"Alright," he said. "See you tomorrow."

And that was that. He told me to report to the Bradenton office.

I showed up the next day, to a decent sized office building. They introduced me to everybody. Other than the attorney who had interviewed me—who did personal injury trials, and usually worked at the other office—the firm I'd be working at included the owner, the office manager, and another attorney who was in his forties or fifties. He was a presuit lawyer; he did not do much litigation. It wasn't like Reed & Reed, in the sense that we're all family, but they had all been working together a long time and were all friends.

My office was on one side of the building, about fifty feet away from the presuit lawyer's office. The firm assigned me approximately fifty files, and told me to start learning them. I had no clue what to do—seriously.

The internet back then was not like it is today. You couldn't just type in a question and get an answer. So I asked a *lot* of questions. But I liked it there; they were all friendly. The office manager did a lot more than just manage the office, so we would talk a lot and became friends. The presuit lawyer and I also became friends. The attorney I'd interviewed with was over in St. Pete, so I didn't see him as much as the others, but we were friends, too.

Whenever a call would come into my office, the people would tell me what was going on or ask their question or whatever, and I would say, "Hold on one second." Then I'd put them on hold and literally run over to the presuit lawyer's office for help. I'd tell him what was going on, he would explain the law, etc., and then I would run back and pick up the phone: "Sorry about that..." and finish my conversation.

That went on for weeks, if not months, while I was learning how to be a personal injury lawyer. God bless that presuit lawyer. To say he was invaluable would be an understatement. There's nothing worse than that pit you get in your stomach when you don't know what the heck you're doing. To humans, in general, the fear of the unknown is almost a phobia. The drive to work was almost an hour, and as I got closer to the building, I'd start getting anxious... because I didn't know what I was doing! And what would I do if that other lawyer wasn't there one day? I'd just have to say, "Oh, I'm not available. Leave a message." Ha!

So that's how it all started. I cut my teeth at that firm, with a heaping dose of help from that older presuit lawyer.

Then, at some point—it was almost like trial by fire—there was a new case and the St. Pete lawyer came in and said, "Hey, you're gonna try this case in two weeks."

I literally went and threw up.

You know what I knew about a trial? Very little. I got to second chair on a few trials, but that is not the same as being the lead trial attorney. They don't teach you how to do trials in law school.

Thank goodness for Perry Mason!

It was a car crash case with liability issues—a lot of car crash cases focus on compensation for injuries, but in this one, proving who was at fault was also a problem—and the client was... let's just say *interesting*, at best. For three days, during the trial, the husband played on his computer and never looked up, never acted like he cared about the trial at all.

Also, come to find out, the defense attorney I was up against was probably one of the best lawyers in Florida at the time. I barely slept for the next two weeks preparing for my first trial.

On the Monday morning the trial was supposed to take place, I showed up and reported to the judge's chambers. I was sitting in a chair outside chambers, waiting, and the defense attorney still wasn't there.

Eventually, the bailiff came out, and said everyone was ready to begin. He asked, "Are both attorneys here?"

I said, "No. [The other attorney]'s not here."

Just then, the judge came out. "I have good news and bad news," he said. "Which one do you want first?"

"I'm a *good news* kind of person," I said.

So the judge said, "Well, the good news is, you're not gonna have to sit in this courtroom the next three or four days."

"Why not?" I asked.

"Well, the defense attorney went to New Orleans over the weekend"—that's how concerned *she* was about this trial, while I hadn't slept for a week—"and she ate some raw oysters, and now she's in the hospital with severe food poisoning."

He told me that, and I swear—I walked straight to the bathroom and threw up again. (I tossed the ole cookies more than once back in those days.) The trial got pushed out a month, which prolonged the stress, but in that moment, the relief was extreme. I felt like I'd been up in front of a firing squad, and they'd just said, "Oh, we don't have any bullets! We'll catch you next month instead."

So anyway, a month later, the trial actually happened. I was kind of like a boxer trying to pop here and pop there, trying to get a lick in, but I had no chance.

The one thing I did well was in my cross-examination of the defense's medical expert. I noticed that he cited the American

Medical Association (AMA) as an authoritative text on his report, yet he was denying that my client's injury qualified as impairment. So when I cross-examined him, I asked him, "Doctor, wouldn't you agree that the AMA guide for impairments indicates that a herniated disc rates a 5 percent permanent impairment?"

He said, "I don't go by that."

So I handed him his report: "Read page three. What is that?"

He said, "It's a citation."

"For what?"

"The AMA Guide for Impairment."

"So is it an authoritative text, or isn't it? Are you in the business of citing non-authoritative texts and trying to utilize them as gospel?" I turned to the judge. "Your honor, I move to strike Dr. So-and-So as a witness."

The defense attorney popped out of her seat then! *Danger, danger—I got a base hit!*

It didn't work, of course, but I felt pretty good about it—I'd gotten a hit in my first game.

I now know that the judge was related by marriage to one of my friends from my college ball days. So after the trial, while the jury was deliberating, he called the defense attorney and me back into his chambers, and he basically educated me. He told me, *This was good, this wasn't; here's what you could do better next time.*

Even the defense attorney was like, "You scored some points with my expert."

So that was my first trial... and it was a disaster, but I learned. Do you know what I learned back then when I won a trial? Nothing, because I thought I did everything right. Do you know what I learned when I lost? Everything, because I would go over the case in my head from beginning to end for several weeks, to figure out what I could do better next time. I tried a lot of cases after that—auto accidents, slip and falls, run of the mill stuff—some with the St. Pete lawyer, some by myself. I was with that firm for four years, from 1996 to the end of 1999, and like I said, I cut my teeth there. It was where I truly became a lawyer.

CHAPTER
SEVEN

Keith Interlude #8: The Wreck with Bundy & Smitty

Back in the day, they had something called bottle clubs. (I don't know if they still do, to be honest, because I'm old.) If the regular bars shut down around two or three in the morning, you could go to these bottle clubs and they'd give you ice, cups, and a mixer; you would bring your own liquor. They were pretty big back then, a way of getting around the laws requiring bars to close at a certain time of night. There were certainly one or two bottle clubs in Brandon.

So anyway, this was in '97 or '98, around when I was working at the firm I just mentioned, when Keith was in his early thirties. Keith had gone out with his friend Smitty, and another guy (we called him Bundy, like Al Bundy, because he was a big, burly guy). That night, they'd gone to Ybor City, partying there until it closed. When Ybor shut down, they headed to the bottle club in Keith's black Ford Escort. The three amigos had a buzz, to say the least.

As they made their way to the bottle club in Brandon, they came upon a curve in the road on Providence. On the east side of Providence was a very deep ditch— eight to ten feet deep—with a little roadway leading from Providence to a little TECO substation. A little bridge, if you will.

Keith was speeding on this pitch-black, wet road, and as he sped through the curve, he lost control. Shocker, right?

Luckily, he was going so fast that instead of going down into the ditch, he hit the side of it. It shot him over the little TECO path, then down into a part of the ditch that was filled with water.

There was no one around.

Smitty had been in the back seat sleeping. He woke up to a dislocated shoulder.

Bundy was in the front seat, but didn't have a seatbelt on, and he was screaming—come to find out later, he'd snapped his legs.

Keith had hit his face on the windshield (seatbelts were not a thing back then). Keith was a savvy veteran of driving with too much alcohol in his system, so he knew he couldn't have the police rolling up on him as the driver.

Believe it or not, to be charged with a DUI, they have to be able to put you behind the wheel while driving. Even in a one-car crash, if you get out of the car and start walking down the road, without proof or witnesses, they can't charge you.

Keith was messed up. His chin was literally hanging off. So he toppled out of the car into the water. Later, Smitty said Keith was drowning. Who the heck knows, right?

Anyway, Smitty heard a gurgling and saw Keith face down in the water. Despite his dislocated shoulder, he dragged Keith out of the water. Smitty then found a tree limb, grabbed onto it with his injured arm, and tried to pop his arm back into the socket. If that isn't a Brandon redneck maneuver, what is?

Meanwhile, Keith was crawling up this ten-foot embankment. Bundy was still screaming in the passenger seat with his snapped legs. Somebody called 9-1-1. It was not Keith, Smitty, or Bundy, I can tell you that.

I don't know how they all got to the hospital, to be honest. But of course, I got a call at 4 a.m. from the hospital: "Is this Paul Reed?"

"Yes."

"This is Nurse so-and-so from Brandon Regional Hospital."

So I was like, "What's up?"

"Well, your brother's been in a crash, and we need you to come to the hospital."

I thought, *Oh no, is he dead?* I guess he'd put me as his emergency contact. So I was like, "I'll be right down." Keith was a frequent flier at Brandon Regional Hospital.

I was still living with Mom in Sun City Center. By the time I made it to the hospital, I heard Keith yelling, "Leave me alone! Get away from me!"

He was talking to the Florida Highway Patrol trooper, who happened to be a guy he and Smitty had gone to school with. He was a guy of small stature, and Keith used to pick on him. (That is called bullying, nowadays.)

Smitty's mom was there with Smitty by then, and they were in one ER room. Bundy was in another ER room. Keith was just wandering around the hospital outside; he just wanted a ride home. Mind you, his chin was hanging off.

I heard Keith and the cop going back and forth:

"Reed, I know it was you who was driving!"

Keith shouted back some expletives.

And so on.

I heard the cop go in and ask Smitty who was driving. "I don't know. Leave me alone."

God bless friends—none of them were driving, and none of them knew who was driving.

That really pissed the cop off, but there was nothing he could do.

So I found Keith, because I could hear him.

He said, "Okay, you're here. Good, let's go home."

And I was like, "Dude, your chin is hanging off your face! I'm not taking you home!"

He said, "Mom can sew it up. Mom can fix it."

That was always Keith's thought: Mom can fix it.

I said, "Mom can't fix that! Go back in there!" I got him in one of those little curtained rooms and said, "Sit down."

Then I popped in to see Bundy, because he didn't have anybody there. He had a knot on his head bigger than a golf ball; he must've eaten the windshield, too. They had a blanket on him; he was probably in shock.

He said, "Hey, man. How do I look?"

His feet were pointing out at ninety-degree angles. But I was like, "You're alright! You'll be okay. Where's Smitty's room?"

"Next door."

I went in next door, and Smitty was sitting on the bed with his mom behind him.

I said, "Hey, Smitty. You alright?"

"Yeah, I'm alright," he said.

"Hey, Ms. Smitt," I said. "How are you?"

She glared at me—it wasn't me she was mad at, but if she could've killed Keith, she would have.

I said, "I'm gonna leave you two."

At some point, they sewed up Keith's face, and we went home.

You'd think Keith would've learned not to drink and drive, from this.

He didn't.

Becoming a Lawyer

Keith Interlude #9: Undercover Drug Bust

I found out about this one after the fact, but during this time period, Keith and his friend Dave lived in some apartments behind Brandon High School and Long John Silvers, around Kings and State Road 60. (I think those apartments are still there.) Anyway, Keith was—apparently—selling marijuana out of his apartment.

On the day this occurred, Smitty and Dave were both there, too. Just by way of a picture, Dave had this little, red car with a hand-painted skull and crossbones on the hood. He was kind of a wild child, and he was living with Keith. Smitty was just visiting.

It was a small apartment—just the living room and one or two bedrooms, a bathroom, and a kitchen.

Smitty and Dave were on the couch playing Nintendo or whatever, smoking dope. Keith was on the phone.

There was a knock on the door, and Keith wasn't paying attention, so he opened the door—

It was undercover cops, in full masks and regalia, guns drawn.

Keith dropped the phone, and was trying to shut the door, trying to hold them off—but there were four cops, trying to force their way in, so of course he couldn't stop them.

They came in.

So Keith was like, "You got a warrant? If not, get out!"

But they weren't leaving. They said, "We know you've got pot, Reed, so either give it to us, or we're going to arrest your two friends right there."

Keith, being the loyal friend he was, went and gave them a quarter-pound of pot, and he got arrested.

So then there was a hearing for the motion to dismiss charges, based on violation of Keith's fourth amendment rights.

Keith went to the hearing, and Smitty and I were there, watching.

Now, the judge had a reputation for being hard, but he was fair. You didn't want to be in front of him for sentencing, but if you wanted a fair shake, he'd give it to you.

So we got Keith a lawyer, and they went before the judge. In the first hearing, the cops just lied. At first, they said Keith consented to the entry, but it became clear that he did not (he was

CHAPTER SEVEN

117

trying to shut the door).

But the judge said, "Well, I'm sure that three officers from Hillsborough County wouldn't come in here and lie, Mr. Reed, however, I'll give you probation and community service." (Kind of like, *Well, yeah, they violated your fourth amendment rights, but you had the pot, so the ends justified the means.* That shouldn't have happened, but it does.)

Keith appealed it, but he lost.

Keith Interlude#10: Keith as a Star Witness

While I was at that firm cutting my teeth, my brother Keith was placed on house arrest for some other charge. I think it was that DUI with serious injury, the one where he totaled my car after leaving Holly's party.

Around that same time, one of his buddies who lived nearby was charged with a serious crime... It turned out that Keith had violated his house arrest by going to a New Year's Eve party at that guy's house. Gina and Keith had gotten drunk at the party and upset some of his friend's guests. Besides getting drunk, Gina had been dirty dancing at the party, which was intended to be a family event, so his friend kicked Keith and Gina out. That angered Keith.

So anyway, Keith got a call from his friend a week later. His friend was freaking out, telling him that the cops had just been there, accusing him of this extremely serious crime. And he told Keith, over the phone, what he'd actually done. This was the sort of crime where you go to jail for life!

Keith was still mad at the guy, but he told his friend to call me. At the time, the St. Pete lawyer at the firm did criminal cases as well as personal injury, so I helped Keith's friend set up an appointment to meet with him. He took the case. But meanwhile, because Keith was still pissed about whatever happened at that party, he called the state attorney's office and told them that his friend had confessed to him.

Now, there was little to no evidence of this crime, only the victim's testimony... so that made Keith the state's star witness.

And the St. Pete lawyer I worked with was defending Keith's

friend.

At some point, there was litigation and discovery going on. I was helping the other lawyer, and we'd done a pretty good job on the case, as far as anything not related to Keith. There was a lot of doubt over the victim's testimony, which led to reasonable doubt about our client's guilt.

It was down to Keith's testimony.

When it came time for Keith's deposition, he showed up to the court reporter's office, and he was drunk. I could see it as soon as he walked in.

We were all there: the court reporter, the St. Pete lawyer, and me. I leaned over to the St. Pete lawyer and said, "Keith's hammered."

He asked, "Are you sure?"

"Oh yeah." He's my brother; I could tell.

We all sat down, and the St. Pete lawyer asked Keith, "Mr. Reed, have you been drinking today?"

It was like 1 p.m., and Keith said, "Oh, yeah, I just had lunch, and I had a beer."

The court reporter asked, "Did you say *a* beer?"

"Well, two or three pitchers," Keith said.

The St. Pete lawyer and I laughed.

The St. Pete lawyer then asked, "Mr. Reed, do you think you're mentally in a position where you can testify today?"

Keith said, "I don't know. What do *you* think?"

So of course, we had to discontinue, because you can't depose a drunk guy—anything he said would be inadmissible.

We rescheduled, and the St. Pete lawyer told the state attorney to ask Keith not to show up intoxicated next time.

People think that things are rescheduled for the next day, like on television... but that's not how it actually works. It can be weeks, if not months, between dates for these things.

Weeks went by, and finally we were back for the second attempt at Keith's deposition.

Keith showed up, and he was pilled out. He had taken *all* kinds of pills; I could see it. I leaned over to the St. Pete lawyer: "Keith's messed up again."

"Drinking?" he asked.

"Nah," I said. "I bet it's pills."

We all sat down, and the St. Pete lawyer asked, "Mr. Reed, have you had anything to drink today?"

Keith looked right at him and replied, "Not a drop. The state attorney told me not to drink anything before the depo."

But his eyes were constricted (pinpoint in size), he was slurring; you could tell he wasn't right.

The St. Pete lawyer asked, "Well, have you done any drugs today?"

"Yes."

"Well, why?"

"My back hurts."

"What did you take?"

Keith started listing oxycodone, Vicodin, just on and on.

The lawyer asked, "Do you think you're fit to testify?"

Keith said, "What was the question?"

You can't make this stuff up.

That deposition got canceled, too.

Several more weeks, if not months, went by. And then we were back for the third attempt.

This time, Keith's attorney had told him, "Don't drink, and no drugs. You need to be sober for this deposition." So Keith walked in, and he looked sober.

The court reporter swore Keith in and the deposition began: "Mr. Reed, have you had anything to drink today?"

"No."

"Have you done any drugs—illicit *or* prescribed?"

"No."

The St. Pete lawyer said, "Please state your name."

Keith said, "I take the fifth."

The lawyer was like, "You can't take the fifth on your name. How is that incriminating?"

Keith replied, "I don't know, *you're* the lawyer. You tell me. Is it incriminating?"

So the lawyer kind of sighed, and said, "Okay, well, I know who you are. What's your address?"

"I take the fifth."

Remember, Keith had been on house arrest at the time... He

knew if he testified that he'd gone over to his friend's house, he'd incriminate himself.

And Keith wasn't stupid. Keith was the guy who had represented *himself* at a DUI trial and got one of our doctor friends to testify that Keith had an inner ear infection which caused vertigo, and that the vertigo was the reason he couldn't walk a straight line and had failed his sobriety test. He'd been his own Perry Mason, and *won*.

So the lawyer asked, "Are you gonna take the fifth on every question I ask you?"

"Yes."

Still, the St. Pete lawyer attempted a few more questions:

"Do you know _____?" (The friend's name.)

"I take the fifth."

The deposition was stopped at that point.

The St. Pete lawyer then filed a motion to exclude Keith as a witness.

The state lost its mind over that—Keith was their star witness, and there was very little evidence to convict the Defendant on. So, the state ended up granting immunity for anything Keith said during his deposition... and there we were, back at the deposition again.

This time, Keith talked.

In the end, we managed to get our client lessened charges based on the reasonable doubt of the victim's story, but Keith's testimony didn't do our client any favors.

The real thing of note here was Keith's deposition itself.

During his depo, Keith threw out info on two or three *other* crimes that he'd either committed or been involved in... that they then couldn't prosecute him for, because he'd been granted immunity for "anything he said during the deposition." It was actually genius.

Like I said, Keith might've been "dumb," so to speak, but he wasn't stupid.

On a final note, I was a pariah to my family during all this, because I could've been responsible for Keith going to jail for violating house arrest. Fun times!

CHAPTER
SEVEN

An Interesting Thing About
Criminal Law

Keith's testimony was pretty condemning, but with how angry Keith had been at his friend, I never could know for sure if he was lying or not. These things aren't always as cut and dry as they seem.

One of the standards for criminal law is that you never ask your client, "Did you do it?" Once you know that answer, you can't present any evidence to the contrary, because it would be a lie. So instead, you say, "Tell me what your position is, and I will do my best to fit my case into that narrative."

Most lawyers take being a lawyer seriously; most lawyers believe everyone is entitled to his or her day in court. But you don't get your day in court if you can't find a lawyer who is willing to represent you, even if they believe you're wrong. And I don't just mean criminal law. This also applies to first amendment issues, or whatever. Some lawyers just can't do it.

There have been insurance defense lawyers who have tried to change sides and become plaintiff's lawyers, and they just can't. They've been in the defense industry so long, and they drank the Koolaid that all plaintiffs are faking it or just in it for the money—and that's just not the truth. Of course there are people who fake things, but I've found as a personal injury lawyer that most people really are telling the truth about their injuries. The fakers are more rare than you might think.

So some attorneys cannot represent certain types of clients, because of their ideology. Not to toot my own horn, but if you hand me a case, I could be the attorney for the plaintiff, or I could be the attorney for the defendant, and do just as good a job whichever side of the table I'm sitting on. And I think the attorneys who can do that make the best lawyers.

Chapter 8

The Next Few Years

Battling Bullies

I joined the next law firm I worked at, in Tampa, on December 15 of 1999. I was still working down at the previous firm in Bradenton that December. The owner had just gotten married to a young banker, and I guess she thought most of us were overpaid. One by one, everyone in the office was let go. I was basically the last man standing.

The owner used a "sign-up boy." (That's just what we called it; he was the one who, when a client called and said, "I want you to represent me," was sent to the client's house to have them sign the contract and medical release.) It wasn't unusual for firms to use a "sign-up boy." In fact, that guy provided the same service to more than one law firm.

There was a Christmas party at one of the court reporters' offices that December (sometime before the fifteenth), and at that party, the owner of the Bradenton firm came up to me and was talking about life changes, moving on, etc.—just acting kind of weird. But I knew he'd gotten rid of everybody else, and my time was coming. The "sign-up boy" and I talked at the party, too, and we both agreed that my days were numbered at the Bradenton firm. The "sign-up boy" mentioned that one of the firms he worked with in Tampa was looking to hire somebody. He connected me with them. I sent in my resume, met with them, and they hired me.

We were all pretty young when I started working there—the owners of the Tampa firm were just a couple years older than me.

Because I'd tried cases with the Bradenton firm, I knew what I was doing, so I became a trial lawyer for the Tampa firm.

Here's the thing about personal injury trials:

Basically, there are two types of cases—*good* cases, and cases that aren't so good. But it's important that the insurance companies know you'll still file suit on those cases that are marginal at best and take them all the way to trial (that you'll make the insurance company spend money, rather than just accepting the insurance company's $500 lowball offer or whatever). You have to try those marginal cases, even the ones the insurance companies think are slam dunks. In my opinion, if you don't, that's just bad business. You will never make as much money as someone who does; it's really that simple... but it's not just about how much money you make. It's about zealously representing your clients. They are counting on you. And it's also about making sure the insurance companies know they can't just do whatever they want.

Insurance companies have to know that there is a good trial lawyer in that firm who will try cases—even if it's just one person. In the personal injury world, we like to say insurance companies try their best cases, and we try our worst. Not to toot my own horn, but I won many of those marginal cases. I could go on and on about some of those cases, but that is fodder for another book.

Well, maybe I'll share one or two.

I was at a mediation once, and there was a liability issue against my client. He ran a stop sign in a store's parking lot. Maybe you've seen those big building supply store trucks. They have the big, long, flat beds with forklifts attached to the back that they can lower when they need to unload. Well, in this case, the driver from the store had backed the truck up right next to the stop sign, and blocked it. My client blew through the stop sign because he couldn't see it, and he got hit. His injuries were severe!

After a year or so of pre-trial discovery, the case was mediated. There were several people at this mediation: the client, the insurance company adjuster, a company representative, three other lawyers representing the store, and me. One of the lawyers representing the store was young, probably cutting his teeth like all lawyers have to do. It's the nature of the beast.

At a mediation, the Plaintiff goes first. The attorney representing the Plaintiff tells the mediator their side of the case, then the other side tells their side of the story. After both sides present their respective cases, they break up into different rooms.

So I was telling our side of the story, and I forget how I led into it, but I said, "I've won cases that I thought I should win. I've lost cases I thought I should win. I've won cases I thought I should lose. But here's what I know: if the jury likes the Plaintiff, then they're more apt to award money than if they don't. It's like this: If you like your neighbor and his house is on fire, you'll run in to save his dog or cat. If you don't like your neighbor, you may not even pee on the fire to try to put it out. That's no different than a jury. If they like my client—and he's a very likable man—then we've got a shot. Now, I've lost my share of cases—"

The young lawyer kind of laughed.

So I said, "Well, it takes nerve to admit in front of a client that you have lost cases. But you know what I learn when I win a trial? Nothing. I did everything right, I'm the greatest lawyer who ever lived, and I won. You know what happens when I've lost a trial? For a month, I go over what I did wrong, and what I could've done better to win. So you tell me... is it better to win a trial, or to lose a trial? When it comes to what makes you a better lawyer, I don't know the answer."

They were silent.

Then I said, "But we're here in good faith."

The case settled at mediation.

If you just don't bull$%&# anyone at a mediation, if you just shoot straight, with confidence—then the people on the other side usually respect that. After all, you're the one who's going to be talking to a jury of strangers if you go to trial, saying what you just said there, only more in depth.

Often, the lawyer from the defense doesn't know the insurance adjuster. They may have sent them memos and reports, but only have met them the day they flew in from wherever for mediation. They may or may not have ever talked to them before.

So, in another mediation while I worked at that Tampa firm, the other side's lawyer told the mediator, "There are lawyers who sit on the other side of that table whose butts I couldn't drag into court with a bulldozer. But that's not Mr. Reed. Mr. Reed will willingly walk through those doors and try a case. And he will try a *good* case. I've tried a case with Mr. Reed, myself. So I think we should all work to resolve this."

If a personal injury attorney doesn't have *that*—that reputation for a willingness to try cases, and to do a good job at it—then they're just peeing into the wind in this business. That willingness to try cases and try them fiercely is what keeps the insurance companies from just bullying people because they know they can.

Remember, you have two choices in a personal injury claim: you either accept their top offer, or you ask a jury to award you what they think is fair. That's it. There are no other options: accept an offer, or try the case. If you can't try the case, and the insurance company knows it (and they do), do you think you're getting top dollar? Of course not—the insurance company can give you whatever lowball offer they want, and you can't do anything about it!

So that's what I'm saying.

In my days at that Tampa firm, I tried a lot of cases, and that was good. I got a lot of experience.

I even got to do appeals. That's where three judges are sitting up there like you see on the Supreme Court, and they fire questions at you. You're sweating bullets, because either you won the original case but they think the judge did something wrong, or you are the one trying to show that the judge did something wrong. Either way, you're trying to defend your position.

Not everybody can do that—it's not easy to be a trial lawyer. What's one of the top fears, across the board for most people? Talking in public. Trials are the epitome of talking in public, with the added bonus of people intentionally scrutinizing every word you say, looking for loopholes or mistakes. Add to that a heavy dose of confrontation, and a side-serving of improv since you have to respond on the spot to whatever the other side throws at you. I'm telling you—trials are a young man's game. When I'm preparing for a trial, I lose sleep. I might stay up several nights in a row, researching, getting everything ready, because I'm not gonna go in unprepared.

So working at that Tampa firm was a lot of stress—high volume, big payroll, big advertising. But I also got a ton of experience.

I worked there for about twelve years, and in that time, I saved a lot of clients from being bullied and lowballed by their insurance companies.

I consider that a good trade.

Just a bonus photo to show that the "Band of Brothers" and I did keep in touch! From left to right: John Simpson, Kendal Luke, me, John Coburn, and David Froneberger. Photo taken in Vegas in 2004.

CHAPTER
EIGHT

Keith Interlude #11: You Can't Do That! I'll Get Disbarred!

Keith lived at 108 Rosier Road, my grandparents' house. I was working as a lawyer by this point—I remember the olive green suit I had on. I might've been coming back from a meeting or something, and it was lunch time, so I stopped by Keith's.

We drove up to a bar in a little strip mall right there on the southwest corner of Parsons and Windhorst—a bar Keith could walk to and from (which was good!) so he went there often. It had a little pool table, the bar, and just a couple of tables with chairs. It wasn't very big.

Anyway, we were sitting there, and I wasn't drinking. We'd just ordered some food when out of nowhere, a guy came up with one of those big glass pitchers, and smacked Keith right upside the head with it. No warning, no anything.

I was like, "Crap! What just happened?!"

Keith was rocked back; it happened so fast.

I don't know how Keith didn't get knocked out. His head was shooting blood like one of those Saturday Night Live skits, but Keith was like a pitbull—if you came at him, you'd better kill him or you're screwed.

Keith jumped up, grabbed the guy, pulled him over to the pool table, and just started ramming the guy's face into the metal corner of the table.

By this point, you couldn't see Keith's face. He was bleeding like he was in WWE wrestling, and the guy's teeth were falling out.

I jumped up and I was like, "Keith! Stop!"

Keith didn't stop.

So the bartender jumped over and grabbed Keith. "Keith, you gotta stop!"

Keith just dropped the guy, then started kicking him.

I was like, "Keith, you're killing him!"

The bartender said, "Go, get outta here!"

I dragged Keith out, and we left. I was like, "Keith, you can't do stuff like that! I'll get disbarred!"

Keith's eye was split open, and he just said, "Take me to Mom's!"

This time, I was like, "Okay!"

So I raced him to Mom's. It was kinda like *Pulp Fiction*, when the person is dying and they ram the car into the drug dealer's house. I came sliding in: "Moooooom!"

She came out, then took Keith inside and put a couple butterflies on Keith's eye and some ice, and that was the end of that one.

I only had the three suits that I'd gotten from Chicago, and the one I was wearing that night got ruined. There was blood all over it. We tried to get it out with peroxide, but it wouldn't come out. The suit was covered in it from me dragging Keith out of the bar.

Poor Mom.

This was probably one reason Barbara Ann (my mom)

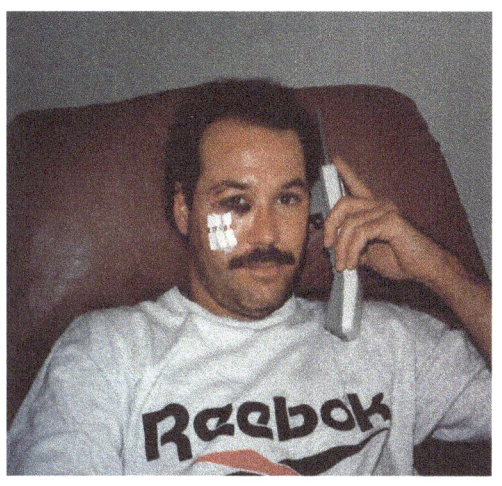

Keith, after Mom patched him up.

moved to Melbourne. When she lived close by, Keith would go over there all hours of the night for Mom to fix things... but when she was three hours away, she could be like, "Sorry, Keith. There's nothing I can do."

Three Steps

Back when I was still working and living in South Tampa, I went to my friend Darrell's wedding. While I was there, I met a beautiful woman named Toni. We'd been talking, and when the wedding wrapped up, I was pretty intoxicated. Since I lived so far away from the wedding location, she invited me to sleep at her house. Nothing else happened. I literally just slept on her floor in the living room. That was it—I went to her house, she went to bed, and I slept on the floor by the couch.

CHAPTER
EIGHT

In the morning, there was a pounding on the door.

I was lying on the floor, hungover, and I was fully dressed but didn't have my shoes on.

Toni came running out from her bedroom. "It's Eddie!"

I was like, "Who's Eddie?"

"My husband."

"You're *married?!*"

She said, "Well, we're going through a divorce."

At this point, Eddie was banging on the door, yelling, "Open up, or I'll knock the door down!"

I was thinking, *Oh no. I'm gonna die. Well, if I'm gonna get in a fight, I need my shoes on.* That was the redneck in me.

I was still putting my shoes on when Toni opened the front door to a guy who looked like the Incredible Hulk. Eddie wasn't very tall, but he was *big*, standing there in the doorway with no shirt on, just a pair of jeans and shoes.

I was like, *Yep, I'm about to die.* So I said, "Look, I don't know what all is going on here. I went to Darrell's wedding—"

Eddie asked, "Darrell _____?" (With his last name, because he knew him, too.)

I said, "Yeah. I had too much to drink, and I live in South Tampa—you can see, right there, I literally slept on the floor. I got no beef, I'm not trying to cut in on anything."

So then Eddie kind of turned toward Toni—

You know that song, "Gimme Three Steps" by Lynyrd Skynyrd? That's what I was thinking, looking for my way out. *Can I please leave?* But Eddie was blocking the door.

Eddie and Toni got into it. I didn't know what was going on, but I knew I didn't want to die. I said, "Eddie, I know you don't know me, but... can I leave? This is between y'all, and I didn't do anything. I slept on the floor."

At that point, Toni kind of pushed Eddie out onto the front walkway. I finally saw my opening, just like in the song—and *Vroom!* I was out of there!

After that night, I don't exactly recall how Toni and I got back in touch—we hadn't exchanged phone numbers or anything after the wedding, but I think I asked Darrell for her phone number to check in on her, like, "Hey, what happened after I left? Are you still alive?" Because I guarantee, when I raced out of there, I did *not* say, "I'll call you later."

Anyway, I remember I got in touch with her a while later, and Toni and I agreed to go to lunch. We met at a Beef O' Brady's in Ruskin or Riverview. Toni was working and lived in that general area, so I drove up from Bradenton, where I worked at the time.

I've gotta be honest: I didn't totally remember what she looked like. It's sad to say that, but this was back when I was still drinking liquor, and I'd been pretty hammered the night I met her. There wasn't Facebook and all that back then where you could look someone up beforehand, so this was basically like a blind date. I was sitting there in the restaurant like, *I hope I recognize her when she walks in.*

There weren't many people in the restaurant, and I was relieved when this beautiful woman walked in and waved at me. I was like, *Phew, alright, good deal. Hey, she's pretty!* "Hi, how ya doing?"

She worked at a church and she'd come from work so was dressed up, and she looked gorgeous. The rest is history. She and Eddie finalized their divorce, and Toni and I started dating.

(Funny point—even though Toni and I also eventually divorced, Eddie and I are still friends.)

LeeAnn

Toni and I got married in October of 1999.

We were supposed to get married a day later than we did, but we had to move the wedding up one day because Hurricane Irene was supposed to hit Tampa. The storm ended up turning at the last minute and cut across the state—it didn't even hit us; the next day was just breezy and partly cloudy. I suppose things never quite going as planned was a bit of a recurring theme for my relationship with Toni, though I didn't realize that at the time.

Our daughter LeeAnn was born on April 7, 2000. Because she was born just after I started with the firm in Tampa, she and Toni used to come visit me at the office, and one of the owners always joked that he helped raise LeeAnn.

I played softball in the firm's employee league, and when Lee-

Ann got a little older, she would come watch us practice on the weekends. To this day, if we run into that owner of the Tampa firm anywhere, he still comments about the day someone hit a foul ball and it went into another field. LeeAnn sprung up and fired right up and down that fence, got the ball, then fired back up the other side and down again, like a little monkey.

Toni and I got divorced in 2008, and from that point, LeeAnn was at my house often. Because of that, LeeAnn and I have a bit of a different relationship than I had with Ryan and Brittany. Of course, I was involved in their lives. Ryan went to Jesuit and played football and lacrosse and wrestled, and I went to his matches. I also coached him in baseball. Brittany played flag football and tennis at Tampa Catholic, and I went to her games and matches, too. However, for much of Ryan and Brittany's young lives, they lived with their mother, and saw me on weekends or here and there in between. But for LeeAnn, I had the opportunity to be much more involved in her life. (And LeeAnn has always been close with Ryan and Brittany as well.)

LeeAnn went to St. Stephen's private school for kindergarten through eighth grade, and from the time she hit about first or second grade, she played every sport available there: basketball, softball, and flag football. When we lived over in Bloomingdale, I coached her in Bloomingdale Little League, too. She was just naturally gifted, very athletic, and good at all of it. I was her flag football coach at school one year, I think it was her senior year, and that year she won Best Athlete at the school. The boy she beat was mad, because it wasn't Best Male Athlete and Best Female Athlete, it was just Best Athlete—and she was. I wish she'd kept playing in high school, but eventually she just lost interest. But for a period of time, I was Dad *and* Coach, and we were doing a lot of softball and other sports.

LeeAnn is grown now—she's twenty-two!—but she still lives with me, and she's still a Daddy's girl.

I'm still close with *all* of my kids, and I hope that never changes.

Ryan's Sixteenth-Birthday Arrest

Ryan turned sixteen when we were living in Fish Hawk, and I had a Mustang I wanted to give him for his birthday—but I wanted it to be a surprise.

There was a police officer living in our neighborhood, so I arranged for him to come over during Ryan's birthday party, in uniform with some of his officer buddies, and act like they were arresting Ryan for burglaries in the neighborhood. The plan was for them to "arrest" Ryan and drive him around the corner to the right, then the rest of us at the party would run around the corner to the left, where the Mustang was waiting with a bunch of balloons and *Happy Birthday* signs. Then the cops would pretend they forgot something and circle back, and "Surprise!" Ryan would get a Mustang. That was my plan.

The day of Ryan's birthday party, all of our family and a bunch of Ryan's friends were there—and the cops knocked on the door.

They handcuffed Ryan right there in front of everybody, and started walking him outside... and my mom started sobbing. She knew it was a setup, so I was there wondering, *Why is she crying?!?* But that only made it better.

The cops drove off to the right as planned, and the rest of us ran to the car... and the whole time, Mom was still crying. By that point, *I* was starting to get stressed. I was like, "Mom, calm down!"

The cops circled back around, lights on and sirens and everything, and let Ryan out. We were all right there at the car.

It was a great way to surprise him—Ryan never saw it coming!

By the way, remember that Tonka truck story? Well, once Ryan got the Mustang, he started driving Brittany and himself over to my place, rather than me picking them up. Every time they'd come over, Brittany would get out of the car all pissed, sometimes even crying, because Ryan drove like a bat out of hell, and she'd say she never wanted to ride with him again!

I guess some things never change.

Brace!!!

In 2005, I was working on an auto accident case. We were using a seatbelt expert located in Long Island, New York. The other lawyers were trying to say our client did not use a seatbelt; we were saying she did. The other side was deposing our seatbelt expert, so I flew to New York for the deposition.

Nowadays, many vehicles have an event data recorder built in (basically a black box), that can tell whether you had your seatbelt on, how much you braked, how fast you were driving—it's pretty amazing how much information they can get just from hooking a car's black box up to a laptop. Anyway, this was before all that, so back then, deposing a seatbelt expert was run-of-the-mill stuff. We didn't always go flying across the country for these depositions, but I'd done it before. It wasn't unusual.

I flew into New York on a Friday, and I took a cab to Long Island. That cab ride cost me about $60 or $70. They deposed our expert, got what they needed to get, then I headed back to JFK or LaGuardia, whatever airport I was using. For the ride back, I decided to take the subway. The subway would only cost me $5 or less, and I'd never ridden on one that was elevated before.

So I was riding that subway or train, whatever you want to call it, and it was pretty cool because I was passing by places like Flatbush, things I'd only ever seen on TV. I remember passing one section of town that was all concrete, a bunch of houses or apartments all crowded together with clotheslines outside. There was this *one* section of grass, maybe two feet by five feet, in front of one house. It was the only grass anywhere in sight. This little old man was out there on it with his water hose, bending over to pick weeds, just taking care of that piece of grass like it was the porch step of heaven. I was also shocked by how many little kids I saw riding that train. They got on alone, wearing their uniforms like they'd just left school, and that blew my mind. Here I was, a grown adult thinking, "Is anything going to happen on this train? Are we safe?" Meanwhile, these kids were getting on the train by themselves, riding to their stops, then getting off here, getting off there, heading on home. Wild.

After about a thirty minute ride, we arrived at the airport, and I got on my plane. I sat in the aisle seat. To my right were two girls, probably in their early twenties if that, and one of them had a baby. So I was making friendly conversation: "Hey, how ya doing? Cute baby." And so on. To my left, across the aisle, were three college boys. We took off, and shortly into the trip—fifteen minutes or so—the pilot came over the speaker.

"Ladies and gentlemen, we've got a sensor in the cockpit indicating there are some issues with the wheels retracting. Sit tight; I'll be back with more info in a moment." (Or something to that effect.)

No big deal. We just chatted and waited.

A few minutes later, he came back on. "We can't fix the problem, so we've got to turn around and go back by the airport tower so they can take a look at it."

It was a Friday afternoon, and I hadn't had a beer yet... But I was like, "Well, okay. Whatever." No one really seemed that concerned about it. Yet.

We returned to the airport and flew by the tower, low, only about fifty feet above the ground. We circled around and passed by it a couple times.

At this point, I was thinking, "This has never happened before. I've never seen a plane do this, not even on TV."

Then, the pilot came back on. "Okay, they've taken a look at it, and they're going to contact us soon. Sit tight; I'll be back on."

About forty-five minutes went by, and everybody was just talking, doing whatever—but I noticed we'd been flying over the water for a long time. So I was thinking, "What the heck?"

I know *now* what was happening: We flew out over the ocean to dump the fuel. But at the time, no one knew that's what was going on.

On the way back, the pilot said, "Ladies and gentlemen, we can't fix the problem, and the tower says they can't tell whether the wheel is locked in position or not"—the wheel was stuck partway down, I guess, and they couldn't just fly like that—"so we need to go back and land, but we have to take emergency preparations."

In case the freakin' plane crashed, because the wheels were stuck halfway out!

Now, people were panicking. The girls were crying, the boys

on my other side were freaking out, and I said, "Whoa, hold up, everybody. I'm from Florida, I just flew up today to do a deposition, and it's Friday about 6 or 7 o' clock—we are not gonna crash. God would *not* take me without letting me have a beer on a Friday night."

They laughed a little, but they were still in panic mode.

I said, "We have nothing to worry about. If I go to heaven today and I haven't had a beer, someone's got some explaining to do." So I was trying to joke around, to calm them down.

Meanwhile, the flight attendants were removing crap. They were taking the little booklets from the backs of the seats, locking the overhead bins—they were preparing for a crash landing.

A woman came up to give instructions. "Everything's going to be okay, but according to the FAA, we have to go through the emergency landing protocol."

So then I was like, *Son of a gun.* I sent a group text to Ryan, Brittany, and Mom:

Hey, we've got a problem here. They've got issues with the wheel, and we've gotta prepare for a crash landing. They don't know what's gonna happen.

We were still too high up for the signal to go through, and it was just an old flip phone, but I hit *Send,* hoping that when we got low enough, it would send automatically.

We flew by the tower real low again, and this time, there were ambulances, fire trucks, and foam all the way down the runway, you know, in case we caught fire.

Now it was like *Crap!* People were just freaking out.

I wasn't externally freaking out, but I was like, *You gotta be kiddin' me! Dying in New York, of all places?*

The girls next to me were crying, and the lady came over and gave them something to strap the baby onto the one girl's chest. It was getting real!

The flight attendants came back by, and if there was anything loose, they took it.

Then the flight attendant said, "Okay, when the time comes—I'm going to say 'Brace.'" Basically, when she gave the signal, we were supposed to put our heads between our legs and kiss our butts goodbye; that's what they tell you to do. I still could not believe this was happening.

We started to land, and the pilot said, "Okay, ladies and gentlemen, we're making our final descent. I'm sure everything is going to be fine, but follow the flight crew's instructions, and when they tell you to brace, brace."

As we were coming down, the flight attendant lost her mind. She started screaming. "Brace!!! Oh $&%! *Brace*!!!!"

Everybody just started screaming, like a scene from a movie. And I saw everyone's head go down.

I was like, "The heck with this! I want to see what's gonna happen! Can I dodge something that's flying by me? If the plane breaks in half, will I have a chance to jump out? I'm not bracing. I'm gonna watch this crap!"

We hit the ground—and of course, we didn't crash—but again, the ambulances and fire trucks were all lined up, foam shot everywhere as I was looking out the window—and we landed. All's well that ends well.

We got off the plane and went into the little seating area. Half the New Yorkers, with their accents, were yelling about how they were not getting back on a plane. Some of them said, "I'm going to rent a car; I'll *drive* to Florida." One of them even yelled, "The heck with Aunt June! She can *die* in Florida! I'm going home!" And off they went.

The rest of us got on another plane, and it was literally half-full. And guess what? They gave us free alcohol.

I finally got back to Florida, and the next day, I said, "I gotta get me a _____ hat," (I'm omitting the name of the airline here, because I just don't want the drama if their CEO ever reads this.) I ordered a hat with the airline's name and logo on it. So, that was that week.

Literally a week later—this one was on the news, with live video coverage and helicopters, etc.—there was a plane from that same airline flying into Los Angeles with the wheel half-down, again. And they *did* land on the nose.

I was like, "Well—ain't flying [that airline] again." And I've never flown them since.

This whole experience kinda goes with what I tell the kids, and even with this business: *You never know.* You get on a plane, a train, especially a car, and you never know if it's that great com-ing-home day. Because you could crash. It's just that simple. You just never know.

But I kept the hat.

Jim Reed's Funeral

Jim Reed died in his sleep on November 21st of 2007. He was an alcoholic, so I can't say we were that surprised, but it was still sad.

I never did form a relationship with Jim, but Keith did. They shared the same birthday, February 28th. At some point, Keith reached out to him, and they started getting together occasionally. Jody and I didn't see Jim much at all, and though we didn't hate him, we barely knew him.

All three of us went to his funeral in Brandon. At the front of the funeral home was Jim's casket. It had a flag on it because Jim was a Marine. Jody, Keith, and I sat on the front row on the right side. Mom didn't go.

The left side was where Jim's *other* family sat. Jim had remar-ried, and he had a wife named Vicky. Vicky had children from a prior marriage. Vicky was nice enough; I'd met her before, at my grandparents' house. But when I looked over at Vicky and the oth-ers, all sobbing... It was just surreal, to be honest. Compared to how they knew Jim, he was almost a stranger to us.

As I said, Jim was a Marine. Toward the end of the ceremony, two Marines came in, took the flag off the casket, folded it up, and handed it to Vicky.

One of the Marines spoke a few words about how Marines don't die, they live forever, and that was the first moment that it really hit me—Wow, someone *died* here, someone who really meant something to somebody. I almost started crying then, because this man they were talking about was my dad, and I didn't even really know him. I felt like I *should* have feelings about his death—loss, or grief, or something—but other than feeling bad for Vicky and Jim's other family, I mostly just felt numb.

My Little Brittany

I often called Brittany "my little Brittany." Brittany went to Tampa Catholic for high school, and her senior year, they offered flag football. At the end of the season, the freshman, sophomore, junior, and senior teams all had a tournament. The football players refereed. Parents came to watch the tournament in the stadium—and Brittany was the senior quarterback.

Brittany was the epitome of a tomboy. She had always been strong and athletic. She could throw the football fifty yards.

Well, the game started and the seniors were on offense. Another girl (one of Brittany's friends) was the wide receiver. The first play after the kickoff, the girl started sprinting down the field.

Brittany hit her with a forty-yard pass in stride, for a touchdown! The crowd went *wild*. The football players were jumping up and down, rolling on the ground, high-fiving Brittany, because they couldn't believe what they just saw her do. The parents in the stands were like "Did you see that play?!?"

Nobody could believe it! And then she went on to have several

---

Game, Set, Match

Brittany also played tennis at Tampa Catholic. Not many parents had the luxury of going to the matches that took place during the day, but I was a lawyer, and I had the blessing of being able to arrange my schedule so I could go.

At one match, Brittany and the other girl were volleying back and forth, and the girl charged the net... She mishit the ball such that Brittany was able to return the volley, and fired it right back at her! It smacked the girl right in the face.

It was the match point, and Brittany won... but the girl started crying.

Brittany, being the good sport that she was, felt terrible. She walked the girl back over to the coach.

But to be honest, the Proud Papa in me was impressed at Brittany's quick reaction in firing it back. I was thinking, "Game, set, match! Way to go, Brittany!"

---

more TD passes that game.

Brittany was queen of the world that day—and I was Proud Papa. I let it be known, "That's my little Brittany!"

Ryan's Twenty-First Birthday

For Ryan's twenty-first birthday in 2008, I flew with him and some friends to Vegas. We had a great time. The night before we were supposed to fly back home, I went back to the hotel to go to bed, because we were supposed to fly out at like 8 a.m.

Ryan said, "I'll be there in a little bit." He and his buddies wanted to go play some beer pong.

When I woke up the next morning, Ryan wasn't there. I called his cell phone: "Get your butt up here! We gotta go!" Then I got in the shower. When I came out, he was passed out on the hotel bed.

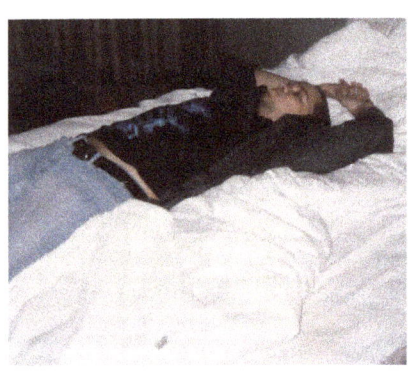

So I shook him awake. "Ryan! We have to go to the airport. Get up and get ready!" I went back into the bathroom to finish getting dressed, and when I came back out, he was throwing up in the bucket.

It was August, super hot outside, and Ryan was feeling like death warmed over—but we had a flight to catch, so we got him to the airport. We checked in, then sat him down near the escalator, where he immediately passed out again.

The way he was sitting near the escalator made him look like a bum. People were putting change in his hand. It was hilarious!

At some point, the airline called us, and we had to get in line. We propped Ryan up in a chair against the wall while we were waiting. Our friend Mark went over and was messing with him. At one point, Mark put a pizza box on his head. (We looked for that picture but could not find it.)

When they finally called us to board the flight, we were like, "Come on, Ryan, time to go!"

Ryan got up and started dragging the chair behind him like it was his luggage.

We were like, "What are you doing?"

By now, people were staring.

Ryan looked down, then back up again, then just kept walking, dragging the chair.

Everyone around was laughing... but then the airline personnel started watching us. The problem was, they won't let you on the plane if you're intoxicated. So we went to Ryan before we could draw any more attention, and got him on the plane. As soon as he sat down, he passed out again.

By the time we got back to Tampa, he was disgusting—he stank, he was hungover, and his hair was all greasy. We got out of the terminal, and there was Ryan's girlfriend, waiting for him.

I handed him off to her. "Good luck!"

Viva Las Vegas!

Pookie Goes to College

I've mentioned that I joked about my daughter Brittany being "Brittany one-ear," and that I called her "my little Brittany," but my favorite nickname for Brittany, the one I called her a lot over the years, was "Pookie."

Pookie (Brittany) was always a little school-phobic. From the first day of school, she just didn't want to go. We kept telling her, "You've gotta go to school."

She ended up attending several different private schools over the years. They were a little smaller than the public schools, and could give a little more attention, so she got through it. She was actually a great student—she now has a BA in International Studies and a BS in Nursing, she went to law school for a year, and she's now working on her Masters. The education component of it was never the problem. It was something about the environment, or maybe she just didn't enjoy being around so many people. Either way, she did not like school.

Case in point—LeeAnn and Brittany both went to the same private school, though not at the same time. Many of the teachers from Brittany's time were still there when LeeAnn attended. One of those teachers ended up telling LeeAnn, "Oh, I had your sister in my class! She never attended school, but she still got all As. Do you plan on coming to class?"

Brittany was living with her mom at the time she attended that school, and if Brittany didn't want to go to school, Brittany didn't go to school. It was that simple. Brittany would just arrange to do her school work at home. So for the four years Brittany attended that private school, if her butt was in her classroom seat even ten percent of the time, I'd be surprised. However, because she was making all As, the school seemed not to mind. Brittany somehow aced all her classes without ever actually going to them.

She was just that kind of person. She even graduated with a full semester of college credit because of Advanced Placement classes.

Brittany graduated high school in 2009. Accordingly, it was time to go to college. Brittany was accepted to Florida State University.

She didn't really express any concerns about it; she actually seemed to be excited about going to FSU. Freshman orientation was on a weekday morning at 8 a.m., about a week or so before school was scheduled to start. Brittany and I drove the four-and-a-half hours up to FSU, which is in Tallahassee, the night before. I got a hotel room nearby at a La Quinta Inn or something like that, about fifteen minutes away. The Freshman students were required to stay in one of the many on-campus dorms the night before. Other than the orientation kids, the dorms were basically empty.

Brittany and I arrived at FSU around 8 p.m.. I dropped her off at the dorm with her pillow, blanket, and a bag of her clothes and stuff. After I dropped her off, I went to get a pizza and some beer, then headed back to my hotel. The plan was for Brittany to stay the night in the dorm, go to orientation the next day, then call me when she was done and I would come pick her up. No big deal, right?

Well, it couldn't have been an hour later—I still had more than half the pizza and some nice cold beer left (I'd only bought a six-pack, so I was not intoxicated by any means)—when I got a call from Kathy: "Brittany is freaking out. You have to go get her!" Why she called Kathy and not me, I don't know. Maybe she thought I would've been angry or something; I'm not really sure. Anyway, I called Brittany.

"Hey, what's going on?" I asked.

She was crying on the phone, hysterical.

I said, "It's okay, relax. Tell me what happened."

"I can't do it. I can't do it!"

So I said, "Okay, look. I'll come get you. We'll stay the night in the hotel, and then we'll go and enroll you at USF tomorrow." The University of South Florida in Tampa was much closer to home for Brittany, and would be less of a change.

Brittany calmed down. "Yeah. Okay." She got off the phone to go gather her stuff.

I put my beer and pizza down, and headed out to go pick Brittany up; by then it was probably about 10 p.m. in Tallahassee.

Well, heck—I remembered the name of the dorm where I'd dropped her off, and I remembered it was a brick building and generally what it looked like, but I didn't know the Tallahassee campus. This was 2009, and I did not have a smartphone yet that I could use to pull up GPS, plug in the address, and get directions to her dorm. If you've ever been to that campus, it's *all* brick buildings. Brick here, brick there, brick, brick, brick. It was like looking for a needle in the haystack.

Finally, I pulled up to an intersection on campus, and there was a guy just hanging out by the road. I rolled down my window. "Excuse me sir, where's—" and I forget the exact name of the dorm, but I asked him where to find it.

He said, "Hey, you wanna buy some crack?"

Now, I needed to find a hysterical Brittany, so I just rolled with it, hoping he'd answer my question. "Nah, man, not tonight. I appreciate the offer, but I've gotta go pick up my daughter and I don't know where the dorm is."

"Oh! Yeah, no," he said, "you just go up here, two lights, hang a right, and it's down on your right. You sure you don't want some crack?"

I was like, "No, but I appreciate it! Good luck!" And off I went.

The guy's directions were accurate, and a few minutes later I arrived at the dorm. Brittany was bawling. After a few minutes, I was able to calm her down. We went back to the hotel. I bought her a soda, she ate some pizza, and we went to bed.

The next morning, we got up, went home, then headed straight to USF to register Brittany there. I didn't care; as long as she was going to college, it didn't matter to me where she went. Brittany seemed totally fine with the whole registration process, and it all went smoothly. Classes at USF were scheduled to start a week or two later. I took her home and assumed everything was fine. She was good to go!

Fast forward to a week or so later. I hadn't heard from Brittany about there being any issues with attending USF, so I assumed it was all fine. I knew it was supposed to be the first day of classes so I called to check in with her. "Hey," I said, "how was school?"

She started bawling "I didn't do it!"

I said, "Brittany, you've gotta go to college."

She said, "I'm just not ready."

Now, remember, she already had one semester of college credit from high school. So I was like, "Well... okay. Then what do you want to do?"

Brittany said she wanted to get out of Florida for a little while. So she packed up and moved to Colorado to live with Mimi and Poppi (Kathy's parents, Brittany's grandparents).

She was out there for close to a year. She got a job working at the Costco as a food sample lady, but the plan was still for her to eventually enroll in college.

I was like, well, okay, she has a semester, so I'll give her some time... but at the end of about one year, I basically said, "Brittany, you have to either crap or get off the pot. You need to go to school, either in Colorado or you need to come back home and do it."

She agreed—she actually *wanted* to go to college—but there was just that barrier of fear.

I said, "Okay, let's do this: Go to HCC. It's a junior college, so it's smaller. It's kind of like high school. You can walk in, sit in the back row, not talk to anybody, get what you need to get from the lectures, do what needs to be done, and leave."

And that's what she did. She went to HCC for two years, then transferred to USF with no issues, and graduated with honors. The rest was history. Her BA from USF is in International Studies, which was a major that really only helped if you were planning to go to law school. Brittany had never really discussed options other than going to law school—I guess maybe she just assumed that since I'd done it, and Ryan, her brother, had done it, it was what was expected. She ended up doing one year of law school at Saint Thomas, the same school Ryan went to. However, she decided she just didn't like it, so she dropped out. Now, if she'd just told me beforehand she didn't want to go, she could've saved me about $100,000, because the school and her living quarters there were *not* cheap. However, a year of law school will teach you a lot. It's not the whole kit and kaboodle, but you actually begin to think differently in one year. So I wouldn't call it a waste, but in the end she didn't like it, and that was that.

CHAPTER
EIGHT

She came home, and I was like, "Okay. Well, now what are you going to do?"

She decided to go stay with her grandmother (my mom) for a couple of weeks in Melbourne Beach, to think things over. As you may remember, my mom was a nurse. Well, guess what—after staying with my mom for two weeks, Brittany decided to become a nurse. I wouldn't have seen that coming for anything!

Brittany is a determined individual. Once she decides to do something, whatever it is, she gets it done. Of course, for her nursing school, she had to take certain prerequisites: Biology, Chemistry, etc. That was about another eighteen months or so of school, but she did it. She took all the necessary classes.

From there, she went to Marymount University in Arlington, Virginia, because they had an accelerated Nursing program for students who already had a degree. That program took her fifteen months to complete. Not surprisingly, Brittany graduated in December of 2019, with honors!

She landed her first job right after, in an emergency room up in Virginia, outside Washington, D.C., in February of 2020... right before COVID. Welcome to nursing! Brittany worked right in the thick of it—in the middle of a plague. What a way to start a career! But did she quit? Not my Pookie. She is still working at that hospital at the time of writing this (in 2022), while also working on her Advanced Nurse Practitioner degree at USF. She actually flies down to take her exams. As always, I'm a Proud Papa! The highly anticipated graduation date is Summer 2024.

The Case That Should've Gone Differently

At some point during my first decade or so as a lawyer, but before starting Reed & Reed—I'm being intentionally vague, for the same reason that we are using no names in this particular story—I served as co-counsel with another attorney on a major personal injury case. Severe injuries!

In this case, our client had his own small business, with just a single semi tractor trailer he used for large deliveries. In this specific instance, he had delivered a truckload of products to a building supply store—the load was heavy and was stacked very high.

The client used tie down straps to hold the load in place. Those kinds of straps are manually attached and detached: you throw them over from one side of the truck and crank them down tight on the other side to hold the load in place. Then during the unloading process, you detach the straps and crank them back up.

Once our client had checked in with the warehouse supervisor, he began the process of unstrapping his load. Our client had removed all the straps except for the last one toward the end of the trailer.

Unbeknownst to our client, as he was detaching the final strap, a kid (an employee) in a forklift came out of the warehouse and decided to unload the truck... without checking where our client was. This turned out to be a huge mistake!

When the kid stuck the forklift through the pallet's holes, instead of going between them like he was supposed to, he misjudged and hit the side of the pallet. As he moved the forklift forward, he dumped the load right on top of our client, nearly killing him.

Now, it was our position in this case that the kid (A) didn't make sure that our client was a safe distance away from the load before he started to unload it, and (B) was negligent when he improperly unloaded and pushed the load over onto our client .

The building supply store denied liability.

Litigation ensued.

The employee's story was, "I checked with [Client] and told him I was going to unload the truck, and that he needed to go to the front of the truck and stand there and wait. I looked under the truck, and I saw [Client's] feet at the front of the truck, so I proceeded to unload. And yes, I did drop the load, but the only reason it fell on [Client] was because he wandered down the side of his truck during the unloading process."

That was the kid's story, and the building supply store was sticking to it.

There was never a pre-trial offer to settle the case. So, we went to trial.

It was a five-day trial. The trial proceeded accordingly, with both sides presenting their evidence, witnesses, experts, doctors, etc. The trial ended on a Thursday. Closing arguments were set for Friday morning. Thursday night, our trial team and the production manager stayed up late into the night preparing for the next day. I mean, we were literally at the office until four in the morning. "Exhausted" would not even begin to indicate how everyone felt!

In a personal injury civil trial, the Plaintiff goes first, and also last (rebuttal). The Defendant argues its case all at one time. So it goes, Plaintiff, Defendant, Plaintiff (rebuttal to what the Defendant just said during its argument). That may not seem fair, but that's simply how it works. Our lead attorney was in the middle of the Plaintiff's closing argument when exhaustion set in. The only way to describe it is like a marathon runner "hitting the wall" (a condition of sudden fatigue and loss of energy). It may look easy on TV, but imagine your brain never cutting off for a solid week, little to no sleep, little to no food (you're just not hungry), battling a worthy opponent all day, and preparing for battle all night... That's really the only way I know how to describe a trial.

Back to the story.

The Defendant's attorney got up next and gave their closing argument. It lasted for an hour, give or take. Contrary to TV, the judge limits how long you can take for closing arguments.

It was rebuttal time. The Plaintiff's number one counsel was exhausted; sweating, breathing deep, heart racing... I literally thought I might be watching a heart attack! There was no way #1 could give the rebuttal. As #1 got up, I pulled him back down. I was like, "No no no, I got this."

As I'd been sitting there, watching the production guy flip through the videos and pictures our other lawyer was using, for the first time, I had noticed something.

We'd been working this case for *years* by this point—like I mentioned earlier, all the discovery and testimonies and mediation and trial dates don't happen back to back; it takes months, if not years, to prepare for a personal injury civil trial.

But somehow, none of us had noticed before that in the security videos, that last little strap was still hanging in the crank at the time of the incident—which proved that our client had never finished untying the load; he'd still been cranking up that last strap, just like we said, when the kid put the forks into the load without checking where our client was standing.

My closing focused on the fact that the bar our client used to crank the strap, or in this case loosen the strap, was still in the strap winder when the load was dumped on the client. There was no way our client was at the front of the truck when the warehouse kid began the unload, unless you believe our client sprinted sixty feet in a couple of seconds. Needless to say, there was a lot more to the story, but that is the gist of it.

Well, that was kudos to me.

The jury went back and started deliberating.

It was finally time to rest and wait for the verdict.

I had a decent relationship with the insurance adjuster. He was a big Red Sox fan, and my brother had played for the Red Sox during his career.

So while we waited for the verdict, I started negotiating with him. "You guys, your story doesn't make sense. You know it; I know it. You heard my closing. The jury has been out three hours... They're just trying to figure out how much money to award the Plaintiff." (Poker isn't just played at the casino.)

So right there, during the fourth hour of jury deliberations, the insurance company offered a settlement of one million dollars!

I was like, "[Client], you need to accept this money."

He said, "No. God is going to provide."

Maybe I need to mention we had asked for $4.5 million dollars during closing arguments. He was waiting for that.

So I launched into a story:

"Tell me if you've heard this one before. There's a flood coming, and a guy climbs up on his roof.

A boat pulls up, and the boater says, 'Hey buddy, climb in! There's a flood coming!'

And the guy says, 'No, no, God's going to save me.' So the boat goes on.

A few minutes later, a helicopter comes by and drops down a ladder. 'Hey buddy, get on! You're gonna die!'

'No, God's gonna save me! Go save somebody else!' So the helicopter flies off.

Then the flood comes, and the guy dies.

He gets to heaven, and he's angry. He says, 'God, I prayed to you, I did everything you asked! Why didn't you save me?'

And God says, 'Dude, I sent you a boat and a helicopter! What more did you want?'"

I said, "[Client], you want God to provide. Six months ago, we'd have settled this case in mediation for $500,000. Today, we're at a million dollars. God *is* providing for you. But I'm fearful that Satan is about to come out that door"—I pointed at the jury box—"and take it all away."

But he still wouldn't accept the money.

Right then, there was a knock on the door. The jury had reached a verdict.

Guess what happened? *Zero.* They found that our client was 100 percent responsible for the incident, and he walked away with nothing.

That was one of those days as a lawyer that you're just like, "I should have gone to medical school."

C'est la vie.

Chapter 9

Hairballs

What Are Hairballs?

"Hairballs" is a term that refers to the pro bono cases I take on. It was given (somewhat lovingly) by our Reed & Reed paralegal, Michelle, because my pro bono cases always seem to spiral out of control and clog up all our office processes.

Though the cases in this chapter occurred *before* we established Reed & Reed, we've applied the term here, as well. To my knowledge—and I know *plenty* of attorneys—it's extremely rare to take on as many pro bono cases as I have taken (and continue to take) on. But I've been blessed with a skillset and the ability to help others, so I help a lot of friends... and because I'm me and I seldom meet a stranger, sometimes I help people first and make lifelong friends in the process. That's not the norm for most lawyers, either, but I make friends wherever I go. That's always been my way.

When we were working on this book, my co-author asked, "Does Michelle call *all* pro bono cases 'hairballs,' or just the ones that spiral out of control?"

I laughed. "They *all* spiral out of control."

You're about to see what I mean.

A Boat and a Scam

One Saturday afternoon, I went to a car dealership in Plant City to shop for a new vehicle. At the dealership, the salesman and I were chatting, and I mentioned that I was a lawyer.

He started telling me about how he was being sued by an insurance company because he damaged his friend's boat.

Now, I didn't know this guy from a man on the moon, but I liked him, and I'd had encounters with the insurance company he referenced. Let's just say I wasn't a fan of that particular insurance company. The salesman seemed like a nice guy, and he was a military vet. So I said, "Dude, I'll help you out." I took on his case pro bono.

I had no idea what I was getting into. This case literally turned into the biggest file I worked on for about two years (unbeknownst to my employer at the time). I had other files I was working on during that time period, of course, but I'd help this client out as new things arose in his case.

So here's what happened:

It was a Sunday, and my client had borrowed his friend's bass boat. It was about a $30,000 boat, which back then was a nice boat. He went over to the MacDill area, put in the boat, and did his fishing.

Coming up Gandy Boulevard on the way home, he got into a road rage incident with another vehicle. Then, my client pulled into a gas station. The vehicle followed, he had some more words with the driver and passengers, then he went inside to pay for his gas. The other vehicle left, and my client finished paying and left, too.

He was driving down Bayshore Boulevard on his way home, nearing the bridge that leads to Davis Island. At that part of the bridge on Bayshore, the road sort of bounces. Well—the boat bounced right off his trailer.

More than likely, the people he'd gotten into an argument with earlier had taken the chains off the boat and unhitched it while my client was inside paying at the gas station.

So, the boat popped off and slammed into one of the bridge's pylons.

There was no real damage to the boat at this point, but the trailer was damaged. My client was there on a Sunday with no way to get the boat home, so he called a tow truck.

The tow truck driver, in his infinite wisdom, decided to pull the boat off the trailer. As he pulled the boat off the trailer, he dragged it on the ground, scratching the bottom of the boat.

Okay, so now the boat was damaged—but it was just cosmetic. The tow truck took the boat to some tow yard... and ultimately, the insurance company totaled the boat. They said the damages voided the boat's warranty, making the boat a total loss. They paid my client's friend $30,000 for the boat, and then sued my client to get their money back for the damage to the boat.

Right away, this story sounded fishy to me. (Pun not intended! But anyway, something wasn't adding up.)

I asked my client, "Was the boat damaged before the tow truck driver pulled it off the trailer?"

"No. The tow truck driver scratched the bottom when he pulled the boat off."

"Was that it?" I asked. "No other damage?"

"Yeah."

Well, that didn't make sense.

So I took his case.

I have a buddy who is an expert in boats. He and his dad own a marine supply store, and they sell and repair boats. My buddy is also a fisherman, and his dad's been in the industry for sixty years—like I said, experts.

I called my buddy and explained the situation, then asked him, "What would it cost to repair scratches like that?"

He said, "You put a sander on it, epoxy it, and the boat's good as new."

I asked, "Would that have voided the warranty?"

"Absolutely not."

"How much would the repairs have cost?"

"$1500, maybe? I'd have to look at it. But nothing major."

This whole situation was starting to look really shady.

I deposed the boat manufacturer that held the warranty and showed the representative the pictures.

"They're saying the warranty was void because of this damage," I told him.

"No," he said. "That would've been fixed with no issue. The warranty was primarily for the two engines, which cost about $15,000 each. We are more concerned about the engines and electrical work. Something that superficial would not have voided the warranty."

I sent that discovery to the insurance company, and I asked, "Where's the boat?"

The insurance company told me, "Well, when we salvaged it, it went to some place in Tarpon Springs."

So I tracked down that place, and I deposed the owner:

"Where's the boat?"

He said, "I don't know."

"Do you still have the boat?"

"No. I sold it."

"Who'd you sell it to?"

"I don't know."

"You don't know who you sold the boat to?"

"No."

I said, "You would agree with me that the boat could have been repaired with some superficial sanding and—"

He interrupted me. "I did that."

"So you repaired the boat?"

"Yeah."

"But you don't have any records on whom you sold the boat to?"

He said, "Some guy in Ohio."

I asked, "Well, did you sell the boat in its entirety?"

"No, I took the two engines off and kept them."

So it went on like that, with him dodging my questions and not providing any real answers... and the bottom line was, they must have had some scam going on. The insurance company claimed the boat was totaled without ever seeing it or inspecting it, then gave it to this guy in Tarpon Springs. After that, the boat just disappeared. I started digging deeper into the scam...

Meanwhile, I was also trying to get my client's auto insurance and homeowners insurance policies to pay for the damages. Both policies had stipulations that should have covered a small portion of the damage related to the boat incident. I looked at the policies, and in my opinion, his homeowners insurance should have covered the loss for $1000, and his auto insurance for about $500. But both were denying coverage... so I brought both of them into the lawsuit. Did I mention this was being done for free and for a guy I met while looking to buy a car?

After conducting discovery, I filed a motion for summary judgment, meaning I asked the judge to rule in my client's favor: "Your honor, here's the policy. It's my position it covers X, and they're saying it doesn't."

The judge read both policies, and said, "Yep. $1000 from you; $500 from you." And that was that.

I had no intention of charging my client anything at all, but remember, by this point, I'd been working on this case for two years. That was a lot of time invested, and it had also accrued some expenses (some of which were on my employer's dime). However, my priority was making sure the suit against my client got dropped.

Now, we had $1500 from my client's two insurance companies. In other words, we had leverage.

I went to the insurance company for his friend's boat, the one that was suing him, and said, "I don't know what the heck you people did, but I've got $1500 that my client will give you to resolve this case. Otherwise, we're going to jury trial with you *and* the Tarpon Springs salvager. You'll have to explain how you totaled the boat sight unseen, and how it simply disappeared."

They accepted the offer.

But that's not the end of the story... not at all. If you sue your own homeowners insurance company or auto insurance company and you win, they have to pay the legal fees and legal costs associated with the case. I filed a motion to tax fees against my client's homeowners and auto insurance companies, and the judge awarded that, too. Each insurance company had to pay me $10,000 in legal fees.

So my client was happy because the suit was dropped without costing him anything, and I got $20,000 to cover my time and expenses from working the case.

That client and I are close friends to this day. I've helped him with other legal matters and represented his daughter with her motor vehicle crash case.

We're family now... from simply going car shopping in Plant City.

Keith Interlude #12: Why I Stopped Eating Out with Keith

One day during this time period, I met Keith and one of his many girlfriends at Shell's seafood restaurant in Brandon for Keith's birthday dinner. I was in a suit; I had either come from work or a meeting, I can't remember exactly.

Anyway, I showed up at Shell's in my suit, and the place was packed. It was about 6:30 p.m., so it was mostly full of families.

Keith ordered some beers for us. Evidently, "girlfriend" had already started drinking—this girl was an alcoholic; she started when she woke up—and she was clearly already intoxicated.

We ordered seafood.

The food arrived, and Keith's girlfriend started eating with her hands. It was funny at first.

This was long before COVID, so the tables were like two feet apart, crammed in there, all full of people—and everybody was just staring at her.

Keith skiing, in 2011.

She was shoveling food into her mouth with her hands, while all these people watched, and her head just kept sinking lower and lower toward her plate, until finally *bam!* She passed out in her plate of seafood.

Keith said, "Ope, gotta go!" He got up, slung the girlfriend over his shoulder with her face covered in food, and walked out the door.

Shell's has a big glass window in front, and Keith's convertible Corvette was parked right outside where everyone could see it. (Keith used a handicap sticker even though he didn't need it, allowing for prime parking spots).

Keith just walked outside, chucked the girlfriend in the passenger seat, and drove off. Did I mention the place was packed and that everybody was watching?

So I was sitting there in my suit and tie, and suddenly everyone was staring at *me*. What do you say at a time like that? So I was like, "Um, can I get the check?"

That was embarrassing.

I quit going out with them, after that, because stuff like that was routine.

The Perjury That Wasn't

Another pro bono case I worked during this time period was for another buddy of mine. He and his wife had gotten divorced. They had two daughters. My friend's wife moved to a small town on the east coast of Florida, and he lived on the west side of Florida, in Clair Mel. His ex-wife was dating a detective in that small town.

Anyway, things went south with their divorce. At some point, my friend failed to return his daughters to his ex-wife's place by the required time. (The girls were fifteen and seventeen years old at this point.)

Well, the boyfriend wasn't having that, so he convinced my friend's ex to take him back to court.

Here's where things got complicated. I guess my buddy got nervous about the prospect of not being able to see his kids, so he lied under oath about some of the logistics of the night in question. Lying under oath is called perjury and it is punishable by up to five years in a Florida state prison. (Here is a little known fact: Florida State Prisons are NOT air conditioned.) Once busted, so to speak, my friend immediately admitted the lie to the judge, recanted, and explained what had actually happened.

But remember, this was a small town. The police, the judges, everybody knew everybody.

My friend ended up getting charged with perjury. He was sentenced to three years in prison—essentially, the three years until both girls were of age and my friend wouldn't have a claim for custody anymore.

Here's the thing: In order to convict someone of perjury, two conditions need to be met. First, the person must have lied under oath. However, if the person recants and tells the truth, it basically undoes that lie; it no longer counts against them. Second, the lie must have a material outcome on the hearing—meaning that the perjury must directly impact the outcome of the case.

Well, in my friend's situation, those conditions simply didn't apply. The judge knew my friend had lied, because my friend *told* him he lied. Since my friend admitted the lie and then provided the truth to the judge immediately, the false information had no effect on the hearing at all. It simply wasn't perjury, under the law... but my friend was still convicted. (Note: I was not my buddy's attorney during all this. I came in long after the fact.)

So at this point, I tried to help my friend. Not knowing anything about what I was about to do, I filed an appeal. The night before the hearing, I left for West Palm Beach where the Fourth District Court of Appeal was. I got up early the next morning and headed to the court house.

I'm not a criminal appellate lawyer. I had no clue what I was doing; I was just trying to help.

I walked in, and there was a podium where you watch the lights for when it's your turn—green light you talk, yellow light you wrap up, red light you're done.

Right off the bat, I found out I had done something procedurally wrong. They called our case, and immediately the other side said, "Mr. Reed failed to file..." They went on about whatever I'd gotten wrong, something about how this court didn't have jurisdiction to hear the appeal.

So I was like, "Well, your honor, I have to be honest: I'm a personal injury attorney in Tampa. I grew up with this family, and no one would help him... In my opinion, what he did, although it was ruled as perjury, wasn't technically perjury, but if I screwed up, I guess I'm out of here."

I started packing up, but the judge said, "Whoa, hold up, son. Just because one side says we don't have jurisdiction doesn't mean we agree. Let's just proceed, and hear what you have to say."

So I presented a very cogent argument. The other attorney didn't say anything in response—because I was right. Instead, he just said, "Well, we're just gonna stick with our procedural argument, thank you."

My friend's appeal was denied.

They should've said, "No, this wasn't perjury—it's not a criminal offense if you recant and it doesn't have a material effect on the outcome of the case being heard." But they just didn't want to hear it. They all *knew* my friend should not spend three years in prison for perjury; they just didn't care.

Years later, I saw this friend at his brother's funeral. He came over, gave me a hug, and said, "Thanks for trying." It's hard to describe how that made me feel.

Why I Never Turn Off My Phone

Part of our marketing for Reed & Reed is the fact that we are *always* reachable by phone—my clients call me directly on my cell, and I basically always have it on me. There's even a commercial we have on TV, where we're out fishing. I start to walk away, and LeeAnn calls after me, "Dad! You forgot your phone!" then I walk back to get it. It's become part of our branding—we never turn off our phones.

But to me, it's not just a tagline. There is a *reason* I never, ever turn off my cell phone... and it's because of what happened to my best friend, Roy Margison, on October 31st of 2010.

It was Halloween night. Even back then, I didn't usually turn off my phone—the kids might need to reach me, or whatever—but I had read somewhere that you needed to turn off your cell phone occasionally, so it could install updates (at least, that's how phones were back then). Since it was about 9 p.m. on Halloween, I thought, *No one's gonna need me tonight.* I figured they'd all be busy with festivities. I turned off my phone and went to bed.

Little did I know, that night was about to go *very* wrong for Roy.

At 9:44 p.m., Roy called me in a panic.

A few minutes earlier, he had been leaving his house on Branch Forbes road. His house is in the middle of nowhere, and the property is lined with oak trees. The house itself sits way in the back, and there's a fence that extends the length of the property. The fence is built with an opening for the dirt road driveway. It doesn't have a gate on it. The opening in the fence is only wide enough to allow one vehicle to enter or exit the property at a time.

Roy had a few beers earlier that night. At some point that evening, he decided to drive to the store, which was about a half mile away, to get some smokes. This was a little after 9:30 p.m.

As Roy was leaving the driveway to make a left-hand turn, his son Austin pulled up in his pickup truck to come up to the house. Because only one vehicle could fit through at a time, Austin pulled up into the drive as far as he could to wait for Roy to pull out—his truck was about half on the road and half off. His headlights were shining directly in Roy's eyes, plus the other side of the drive was all oak trees. From where Roy was, there was no way to see that there was a motorcycle speeding toward them from down the road.

Now, the motorcyclist had been out all day drinking with his biker buddies. He'd come home earlier, picked up his seventeen or eighteen-year-old stepdaughter, and took her to the Scoreboard Lounge, where he'd continued drinking. Then he decided to go home. When the accident occurred, the motorcyclist was three times the legal blood alcohol limit. He was speeding at eighty miles per hour northbound down this dark road, with his stepdaughter on the back of his bike. The speed limit there was forty-five miles per hour.

Roy pulled out around Austin's truck to head southbound on Bell Shoals Road.

It's unclear what happened next. It could be that the motorcyclist didn't see Austin's truck until it was too late and tried to veer to the left to avoid smashing into the back of it—remember, Austin's truck was half on the road and half off, so the motorcyclist may not have seen his tail lights. Or it could be that the motorcyclist swerved for some other reason. Either way, the exact moment the front of Roy's car cleared the back of Austin's truck, the motorcyclist swerved into the southbound lane, lost control, and crashed directly into Roy's car.

The impact spun Roy's vehicle 140 degrees clockwise and knocked it 200 feet in the opposite direction. His car stopped when it struck a large oak tree.

At 9:44 p.m., I got the panicked call: "Paul, he's dead! He's *dead!* What do I do? What do I do?!?"

Remember, I turned off my phone that night before going to bed. I never do that! So, when I finally turned my phone back on the next morning, I heard the message.

I will never forget that message: "Paul, he's dead! He's dead! Oh my God! Where are you?" I could hear screaming in the background. The girl was still alive. I could not make out what she was saying, but it was a scream I will never forget. She sustained serious injuries from the crash, as one might imagine.

By the time I listened to the voicemail the next morning, it was too late to tell Roy what to do, or what not to do. To this day, I am not sure what advice I would have given my best friend. Would I have told him to run? Would I have told him to tell the police he was not driving? Would I have told him to say someone at the house who was not intoxicated was driving? I guess we will never know. (I usually never turned off my phone. Why that night? Maybe God was looking out for me that night.)

Roy was eventually arrested and ended up being sentenced to four years in prison for DUI manslaughter.

Before I go deeper into how that all played out, I want to mention that Roy was injured, too. It had been a serious impact, plus his car had spun out and hit a tree. The motorcyclist did not have insurance, but Roy had uninsured motorist coverage through his wife, Michelle's, policy. I submitted a settlement demand for the $10,000 uninsured policy limit to the insurance company.

Upon receiving the demand, the insurance company's adjuster called me. He asked why they should tender the policy limits when Roy was being charged with DUI manslaughter? A legitimate question.

My response was short and sweet: "I don't care what the state of Florida is charging my client with. He wasn't at fault for the crash." I explained the details of the crash to him, emphasized the fact that the motorcyclist had a blood alcohol level in excess of three times the legal limit, and was traveling over eighty miles per hour... "This is what caused the crash." They paid the $10,000 policy limits.

In addition to Roy's arrest, Roy and Michelle (Michelle was the owner of the car) got sued by the deceased man's estate, and by the girl who was on the back of the bike. Luckily, Michelle's auto policy had bodily injury coverage. I knew the defense attorney hired to defend Roy and Michelle, and I was able to help my friend hire an accident reconstruction company to recreate the crash. (The accident reconstructionist was also a friend.) To say this was expensive would be an understatement. The reconstructionist company had to buy a motorcycle similar to the one in the accident, a truck that was similar to Austin's, and a car that was similar to Roy's. Then they hired off-duty police to shut down the road from sunset to sunrise. It looked like a Hollywood movie set out there. We were there from sunset until the next morning, running scenarios, and in the end, I had a video and a virtual reality video that showed Roy was not at fault for the crash. The videos showed: *If the motorcyclist hadn't been speeding, the crash would not have occurred. Roy would have pulled into the southbound lane of travel, Austin would have pulled into the driveway, and the motorcyclist would have driven by the house with plenty of room to spare.*

C'est la vie.

DUI manslaughter comes with a maximum sentence of fifteen years in prison. DUI with serious bodily injury also has a fifteen year maximum sentence.

The state attorney knew the crash wasn't Roy's fault, so she said, "Look, if you want to go to trial and win, I don't care. I'll put on a case. If the jury finds you're not at fault, so be it." The detective who investigated the case said about the same—he didn't care if it went to trial. The detective played golf with Stinger so he didn't "have it out for Roy," unlike some cases. Roy had to consider this: if he went to trial and *lost*, he could end up getting the maximum sentence: thirty years in prison. If he pled guilty, he could get four years, which was the minimum.

Here's the kicker: the state changed the wording of the law for DUI manslaughter from "caused the accident" to "caused and/

or contributed to the crash." What the heck does *that* mean?

Here is an example: I am driving down the road, minding my own business, but I'm over the legal limit. (Let me stop and say one word here: "Uber.") Someone traveling in the opposite direction while distracted by a cell phone comes into my lane and we collide head on. If someone in the other car dies, I can go to prison for fifteen years, even though I did not cause the crash. You might ponder, *That's not fair.* Well, the State of Florida would respond, "You contributed to the crash by being on the road." Bummer, right!

The legal limit for blood alcohol level in Florida is .08. If you've had three beers, you're probably over the legal limit. Now, I could probably drive from here to Hawaii on three beers, but that's not the point. You should *not* drink and drive, that goes without saying, but many people don't realize they might actually be over the legal limit even when they aren't showing any signs of being impaired. Just be aware: according to the law, it's not only *your* driving you have to worry about, it's also anyone else who might be driving recklessly, or just not paying attention to the road. Trust me, it's not worth the risk. Just Uber.

Anyway, the judge told Roy, "Look. You could plead guilty, and be out before the next president is elected, or you could go to trial, possibly lose, and there could be *four or more* presidents elected to office before you get out."

Roy said, "Well, I am a gambler... but I don't gamble like that." He took the plea, and went to prison for four years.

But there's more to this story...

The night of the accident, police and EMS showed up at the scene.

The officer at the scene told the EMS firefighter/paramedic, "I want you to draw Mr. Margison's blood."

That's standard at crash scenes like this one. They use the blood to determine if the person had any drugs or alcohol in his/her system. Back then, you didn't need to consent for a blood draw; they could just take it. Since then, the law has been changed to require consent, or a court order. But in any case, Roy consented, so it wouldn't have mattered.

The paramedic drew Roy's blood, and gave it to the officer.

Now, when blood is drawn at a crash like this one, both the

deputy and the paramedic have to watch the blood draw, then it immediately goes into a box which is sealed and signed by both witnesses. Chain of custody is a *big deal.*

Well, in this case, the officer apparently insisted that the box didn't need to be sealed. He left with the blood... and didn't turn it in for several hours.

That then became a big issue with chain of custody: What did the cop do with that blood from the time it was taken from Roy, until the time he turned it in? We filed a motion to suppress the blood as evidence, based on those chain of custody issues. Also, we ended up deposing the paramedic from Hillsborough County Fire Rescue who had drawn the blood.

We found out the cop had gone to the paramedic, to try to get him to lie about what happened. Apparently, the cop had shown up at the fire station more than an hour after he'd taken the blood from the scene, and had asked the paramedic to sign and seal it after the fact.

At first, the paramedic refused. That's significant. Eventually, the paramedic signed the seal of the blood collection kit, but only because he was asked to by the law enforcement officers. He stated that he did so under protest, because he did not know where the blood had been, and believed the blood should have been sealed and signed at the scene of the accident. When he reported what happened to his captain, the captain told him to file an incident report with headquarters. (You can see some of this information in the images I've included from the deposition and our motion to suppress, below. These are all public record, but for the purposes of this book, I've redacted the names.)

G

IN THE CIRCUIT COURT OF THE █████████ JUDICIAL CIRCUIT
IN AND FOR THE COUNTY OF █████████ STATE OF FLORIDA
CRIMINAL FELONY DIVISION

STATE OF FLORIDA,

vs.

████████████

Defendant.

CASE NO.: ████████████
DIVISION:

MOTION IN LIMINE TO EXCLUDE EVIDENCE OF DEFENDANT ████████████'S
BLOOD ALCOHOL LEVEL

The Defendant, ████████ by and through his undersigned counsel, moves this

Honorable Court for an Order In Limine excluding from evidence any reference to the blood

alcohol test results obtained from the Defendant's blood, drawn on October 31, 2010. In support

of this Motion, Defendant states as follows:

I.   FACTUAL BACKGROUND.

On October 31, 2010, Defendant Margison was involved in a vehicular accident. Fire

Medic I, ████████, employed by Hillsborough County Fire Rescue, was at the scene of

the accident and described it as a "jumbled mess," where "everybody got jumbled up." ████

Dep., p. 19.[1] Although Mr. ██ did not ordinarily perform blood alcohol draws at the scene of

an accident, he was requested to take a blood draw from Defendant Margison by ████

████ a Hillsborough County Sheriff's Office Deputy. ██ Dep., p. 9, 22, 25, 26;

Hillsborough County Sheriff's Office General Occurrence Hardcopy.[2] Mr. ██ testified that

Defendant ████ did not appear impaired at the time of the draw. ██ Dep., p.33.

---

[1] The deposition of ████ is attached hereto as Exhibit "A" and referenced herein as "██ Dep., p. ██"
[2] A copy of the Hillsborough County Sheriff's Office General Occurrence Hardcopy, which references ████ ████ is attached hereto as Exhibit "B."

1

4

1 ██████████

2 being first duly sworn to testify the truth, the

3 whole truth, and nothing but the truth, was examined

4 and testified as follows:

5   THE WITNESS: I do.

6   EXAMINATION

7 BY MR. S███████:

8   Q State your name for the record, please.

9   A ████████████.

10   MR. S███████: Can you hear us now,

11 ████████?

12   MR. C█████: I can. Thank you.

13 BY MR. S██████:

14   Q Mr. ████, my name is ██████████. I'm an

15 attorney. I represent a gentleman by the name of ████

16 ████████ regarding an incident that occurred back on

17 October 31st of 2010. I'm going to ask you some

18 questions about what you remember about that incident

19 and that evening. I'm going to ask you whether or

20 not you have an independent recollection as we sit

21 here today about that.

22   A Quite honestly, I've done thousands of

23 automobile accidents and that. This one here, do you

24 have any paperwork that I did?

25   Q I have a -- let me see.

EXHIBIT
A

1   I'll show you whatever you want to see, but
2   do you have an independent recollection as you sit
3   here or do you need something to refresh your
4   recollection?
5   A   Yes, I need to something to make sure what I
6   say is in reference to the proper one.
7   Q   I'll tell you that it occurred out on Branch
8   Forbes Road in Plant City. It was a motorcycle/SUV
9   accident. And I'll show you a police report. I
10   don't know if that is going to help.
11   A   Would this be a dad and a daughter, a man
12   and a girl, and the man passed way, and a guy backing
13   out of a driveway?
14   Q   Well, I wouldn't characterize it as a man
15   backing out of a driveway, but that -- came out of a
16   driveway.
17   Is that what you recall?
18   A   Well, like I say, I've had tons of the
19   strange ones. The next question I have for you, did
20   I do a blood-alcohol draw on the driver?
21   Q   That is what I'm going to ask you. I'll
22   show you this. Just for the record, I'm showing the
23   witness a ▮▮▮▮▮▮▮ County Sheriff's Office Blood
24   Collection Form. It's the short form.
25   A   Was this right outside this person's

6

1 driveway?

2   Q   I will relate to you it was.

3   A   Okay. Then this is no good because -- and I

4 explained to the deputy when I did the blood draw,

5 that I had to witness everything and box it up and

6 seal it together. And I believe an incident

7 report -- that's why I had to go outside. Because I

8 don't have any paperwork, since I'm retired, I don't

9 have access to any of the records.

10   But I made an incident report because the

11 deputy showed up at my station and said that 1 need

12 to witness the box and that. And I said, "I cannot

13 do that because I have no idea where this blood

14 sample has been." I said, "We needed to do that when

15 I was on the scene."

16   Q   Okay. Let's -- let me back you up and we'll

17 talk about that. You just gave me a lot of

18 information. You've just now looked at a police

19 report. I gave you a little bit of information. You

20 looked at the Blood Collector's Report.

21   These items have refreshed your recollection

22 about this particular incident?

23   A   It would be better if I had -- had mine.

24 But, yes, that was the incident that I remember that

25 I had trouble with. And I talked to my captain at

7

1   the station. And I told him, "You know, this deputy
2   is telling me I have to sign this" and -- because it
3   was shortly -- it was shortly after the accident
4   occurred.
5   It was back at my station. And it took me a
6   while to get a hold of my chief. And I made an
7   incident report up.
8   I don't know where the incident report is.
9   And telling him that, "Hey, you know, I have no clue
10   what happened to that blood, you know, from the time
11   I was at the scene and I drew it, until the deputy
12   shows up at my station wanting me to certify it."
13   MR. C████: Can I interrupt you just to
14   make sure that -- because I'm not there seeing
15   what you're looking at, am I understanding
16   that you're showing him the paperwork from the
17   blood kit? Is that what we're talking about?
18   MR. S████: ████, I showed the
19   deputy -- I showed Mr. ████ -- he's looking at
20   the police report itself.
21   MR. C████: Okay.
22   MR. S████: The Florida Traffic Crash
23   Report. And then I showed him -- now, in my
24   discovery, it's -- and I know you and I have
25   had this come up before where our pages might

8

```
1    have been different, but mine is Page 62 of
2    202.  And it's a ▮▮▮▮▮▮▮ County Sheriff's
3    General Occurrence Hardcopy.  And I showed
4    him -- there's a copy of two separate --
5         MR. C▮▮▮▮:  The Consent Form, the
6    investigating officer's report --
7         MR. S▮▮▮▮:  Correct.  That's all that
8    Mr. ▮▮▮ has looked at.
9         MR. C▮▮▮▮:  And I'm understanding from
10   what Mr. ▮▮▮ is saying, that the deputy came
11   to him after the fact asking him to sign these
12   forms?
13        MR. S▮▮▮▮:  Well, that's what we're
14   getting -- that is what it sounds like.  I was
15   going to ask him some more questions about
16   that.
17        MR. C▮▮▮▮:  I just want to make sure
18   that I was hearing this correctly.  Go ahead.
19   BY MR. S▮▮▮▮:
20        Q    ▮▮▮▮, while we're on that -- Officer
21   ▮▮▮▮ is it a -- you said you filled out an incident
22   report?
23        A    Yes.
24        Q    Tell me what the incident report describes.
25        Was it the fact that the deputy came and
```

9

```
1   asked you after the fact or was it --
2       A    Yes.  Yes.
3       Q    The incident report is on whose form?
4       A    It's basically just a typewritten form that
5   I turned in to my captain and it goes to my battalion
6   chief and then it would go to headquarters.
7       Q    Let me back us up a little more because we
8   kind of jumped into this sideways.
9            Who did you work for on October 31, 2010?
10      A    ████████ County Fire Rescue.
11      Q    Okay.  I want to get back to all of this
12  stuff, but to make a clean record, I want to kind of
13  start back from the beginning.
14           How long had you worked for ████████
15  County Fire Rescue?
16      A    Fifteen years.
17      Q    Okay.  And, Mr. ████, what is your
18  position -- I understand you're retired now, right?
19      A    Yes.
20      Q    Congratulations.
21      A    Thank you.
22      Q    Are you employed now at all?
23      A    No.
24      Q    Good for you.
25           What was your title?
```

All of this was a big deal. It was a clear violation of proper chain of custody procedures, and—in my professional opinion—based on that, the blood draw should have been excluded from evidence.

The paramedic also testified that Defendant Margison did *not* appear impaired at the time of the blood draw—so it was very contentious. Whether or not Roy had actually been impaired came down to the blood alcohol evidence. With the chain of custody issues, it was theoretically possible that the blood had been tampered with.

The kicker was, Roy and the motorcyclist both worked for the same company, though they didn't know each other. The word on the street was that this guy drank and drove so much that it was only a matter of time before he got himself killed on the motorcycle. But none of that was relevant to the charges against Roy. He'd been "under the influence" and had "contributed to" the accident, so in the eyes of the state, Roy was guilty... so long as you factored in the blood evidence which showed that his blood was above the legal limits.

(The blood which had mysteriously disappeared for several hours before being signed, sealed, and turned in.)

If the blood evidence had been suppressed (excluded), the whole case against Roy for DUI manslaughter fell apart—the state may well have dropped the charges.

I've known Roy for over fifty years, my whole life. I did everything I could for him, but ultimately, the judge denied the motion to suppress the blood evidence. Instead, Roy spent four years in prison. The law is a fickle beast, my friends.

But that's how it goes. Judges have a lot of power. However, I believe all that doubt about the evidence played a big part in why the judge only sentenced Roy four years in prison instead of fifteen.

I visited Roy in prison often—I wasn't just his lawyer. He was (and still is) my best friend.

This case, what happened to Roy... *this* is why my phone seldom leaves my side, and why I no longer turn it off. You just never know what might happen, and I don't want a call like Roy's to go unanswered, ever again.

I want to be there when people need me.

I can't end this story without letting you know that one Sunday morning— it was a beautiful day, between 8 and 9 a.m.— I was traveling east on I-4 in Polk County when I was pulled over by a state trooper. He was sitting at the end of the exit ramp I took to get to the prison. I asked him why he pulled me over.

He said I was speeding.

I said, "How do you know, given your location at the end of the exit ramp?" He pointed to the sky.

Son of a biscuit eater! The Florida Highway Patrol had an airplane clocking speeds. Eighty-four miles an hour later...

U.S. Marshals, a Drone, and Tax Fraud

The plan was always to open up Reed & Reed with my son, Ryan. I'm not sure how it all got started, but for years and years, that had been the plan.

Ryan graduated from Jesuit in 2006. From there, he went to the University of Florida where he majored in English. You've really gotta be committed to law school, or plan to be a writer or something, to get a B.A. in English from the University of Florida. But for those planning to go to law school, that's what they recommend: *Get a degree in English*, because law school is a lot of reading and writing. Ryan graduated from UF and earned a "free ride" to St. Thomas Law school.

After graduating from law school, Ryan and Jackie, now his wife, moved in with LeeAnn and me. We lived in Valrico. I still worked in downtown Tampa, but now for a different firm.

For the most part, potential clients usually didn't want to come downtown to the high rise office—traffic downtown is a beast—so instead, I'd drive to people's houses, sign them up, and come back. This wasn't a big deal; we still do that with Reed & Reed now, when it's more convenient for the clients.

On this particular day in 2012, I was meeting with a potential client whose minor son had been injured in an automobile crash, and I was going to represent him. So I drove to an area where individuals with social and economical disadvantages lived (take that for a politically correct description of where I went).

I've never felt uncomfortable around or judged anyone based on their income or where they live. Why would I?

But anyway, I pulled up in my car, got out in one of my nice suits, and knocked on the door.

The woman who answered the door was very nice. She had on a long, colorful dress—shades of bright yellow and green—and was heavy-set. She invited me in.

Inside, the duplex was dark, but clean, and it smelled like gonja (marijuana). I sat on the couch across from the lady, and we chatted for maybe thirty or forty minutes. It was pleasant, nothing unusual—and I signed her son up. I got in my car and drove the twenty minutes back downtown to the office.

No sooner had I sat back down at my desk when I got a call from the receptionist: "Mr. Reed, a U.S. marshal is on the phone and would like to speak with you."

So right away, I was thinking Keith did something. *U.S. marshals? Crap, Keith, you're in trouble now!*

The receptionist put a U.S. marshal on the phone, and he said, "Mr. Reed, do you mind if we come to your office and talk?"

I was still thinking this was about Keith, and I didn't want the marshals coming up to the office. I didn't want "family business" brought there... still thinking this had to be Keith. The Bank of America building had a plaza downstairs with tables, so I said, "Well, I don't mind talking to you, but let's do it downstairs."

The U.S. marshal said, "Oh, we don't care where, we just want to talk."

So I went downstairs.

The Bank of America building is right on the corner of Kennedy and Tampa Street, two main streets, and it has big, glass windows on all sides. I made it to the lobby, and sure enough, there was this Lincoln Town Car parked right up front, with blacked out windows, a little light on it, fancy—definitely a cop car. The car doors opened, and out climbed two buff, young guys with their black U.S. marshal vests.

I'm like, *Yep, U.S. marshals, alright. What in the world did Keith do?*

So we sat down at a table, and they introduced themselves.

They were nice guys, and one of them asked me, "Were you just at such-and-such location?" (They gave the address where I'd just met the new client.)

That surprised me, but I said, "Yes, sir."

He said, "Do you mind if we ask what you were doing there?"

So I was like, "Nah, that's fine—I was signing up a new client whose son was in a crash."

The U.S. marshall cursed emphatically.

I said, "What? Why?"

He sighed. "This woman..."

It turned out, this woman and her crew were stealing tax checks from people, like two or three million dollars' worth—I saw that later in the paper—and the U.S. marshals had been about to raid the duplex, hoping to catch her, when I pulled up. They'd thought I was the big fish, the big kahuna behind this tax theft ring!

So the marshals said, "Mr. Reed, we're having a hard time catching this woman. Would you mind calling her and asking her to come downtown because you forgot to have her sign something?"

I looked right at them. "Fellas, I don't think The Florida Bar would appreciate me setting my client up for arrest. God bless you, and thank you. Have a nice day and good luck." And I went back upstairs.

I went home that evening, then back to work the next day. At some point while I was at work, I got a call from Ryan.

He was home studying for the Florida bar exam, and he was out by the pool in the screened enclosure. He said, "Dad, there's been a drone flying around your house for fifteen or twenty minutes."

Now, this was back in 2012. It wasn't common for people to have recreational drones, or to just see one flying around.

So I was like, "Really? Well, go out and act like you're looking at it. See what it does."

Ryan went back out with me still on the phone. The drone was still there, so he went right up toward it. *Zzzzip*, off it flew!

Who do you think was surveilling my house with a drone?

They still thought I was the big fish, and they were watching me!

CHAPTER
NINE

Ryan graduated law school and passed the bar, and in late 2013, I said goodbye to Tampa and hello to Brandon! It was time for a new venture, one I hadn't dared to dream of when I was younger: a family law firm. A family legacy. A chance to establish something that could truly help our hometown and community.

...Reed & Reed was born.

Part IV

Reed & Reed

———————————————————————————— PAUL REED

Chapter 10

Starting Over

Two Desks and a Printer

We started Reed & Reed on October 1, 2013.

My buddy Bob (I'd met him playing baseball at Florida College and we'd stayed in touch after graduating) had become a CPA in Brandon, and he had an office on Parsons near Windhorst. It was this big, brick building on about four acres of land, with one of those fancy digital signs out front. He found out about our plans to start Reed & Reed, and he said, "Hey, for $2,500, you guys can have one side of my building."

It was just a big open space, like a New York City flat, with a little room attached. The small room eventually became Michelle's small office. (She joined us in January 2014.)

Ryan and I were broke—I had about fifty or so clients who had come with me from the previous firm, but most of these cases were still in their infancy. We never knew when something would actually settle and we'd get paid. Needless to say, Bob's offer was a lifeline.

Bob bought us each a desk and chairs, and we purchased two desktop printers. That first day, Ryan sat on one side of the office, I sat on the other, maybe thirty feet apart, and off we went!

So we were sitting there, day one or day two of Reed & Reed, and the mail came in. We had no inboxes, no system for sorting it, so we just spread it out on the floor between us.

I remember thinking to myself, "What the heck have I done?" Ryan was day one as a lawyer; he knew nothing. I'd left a job where I was making $200,000 or more a year, and now here I was, having to train Ryan, and we had little to no money. We were starting from scratch. I secured a line of credit for $50,000 for our safety net—believe it or not, we never touched it.

But $2500 for office space, phone, electric, a nice lobby, and access to a conference room? It was incredible. Bob took care of everything. We couldn't have done it without him.

Most of the calls for Reed & Reed came straight to our cell phones. Bob had a receptionist in the lobby who would let us know when our clients walked in, and Bob gave us access to use the big conference room in the middle of the office building. He hardly used that room, so we basically had free use of it, and to our clients it seemed like we had a nice, fancy office. Little did anyone know, it was just Ryan and me in a back room, with our mail all spread out on the floor!

The phones rang sparingly. Clients would come in here and there, but Ryan and I had a lot of time to kill in those early days. There was only so much mail-sorting we could do, and we didn't have funds yet for advertising. We were working mostly on word of mouth.

During lunch, Bob and I would take twenty to thirty minute walks around the four-acre property, just talking. I gotta say, I do miss our walks. During baseball season, Ryan and I would take gloves and go outside and play catch. Bob would join us on occasion. During football season, we'd throw the football. We even made a little frisbee golf course out there. (Like I said, we had a lot of time.) In the back of Bob's property was a drainage ditch. The walls were maybe six or seven feet high. Ryan and I would take towels back there, lie in the sun, and work on our tans.

Remember, Ryan and his then girlfriend Jackie moved in with LeeAnn and me after graduating from law school, so we all lived in the same house. At the time, Jackie was a lawyer still looking for that first job. She would send out resumes most of the day, then while Ryan and I were still at work, she would go out to the casino and play poker. She would stop by Bob's to see us on her way home, and she would come home with $200 or so from poker nearly everyday. Ryan and I would joke, "Well, you made more money than we did!" She'd use that money to go buy groceries for us, or whatever, and we'd all go home and cook dinner. It went on like that for months. I must say, I do miss those days too!

I remember when we hit our first milestone—the goal was, "Man, I can't wait until we have $50,000 in the bank. Will we ever get there?" We couldn't believe it when we actually did it. It was like, "Oh my gosh!" We even took pictures of the bank statements. Then we were like, "Man, okay... will we ever have $100,000?" And we hit that, too. Those were the goals—not a million dollars. Just $50,000, then $100,000... and it didn't happen overnight. It was at least a year before we had $100,000 in the bank. But from there, it just kept growing. (For you kids out there, hard work and perseverance really does pay off!)

Faces All Over Brandon

After we hit our first milestone, we rented some of those signs you see at the bus stops. That was our first form of advertising.

Our next form of advertisement was the little marquis inside restaurants like Cherry's and Beef o' Brady's.

At some point, Ryan joined a business networking group, and we started getting more referrals. Meanwhile, we continued to invest in advertising.

Next came Bay News 9 commercials... then billboards... then more television and radio, and eventually, also social media marketing.

We started with nothing, and now we have a fancy website, Facebook ads, *Live Feed Reeds* videos on Facebook every Friday, commercials on TV and radio, sponsor booths at rock concerts, and billboards with our faces all over the Brandon area.

I'm as shocked as anybody.

I was born and raised 1.9 miles from where our office is now. (Bob's office is 0.9 miles from where I grew up.) So I told Ryan,

THE OTHER SIDE OF THE LAW

"There are all these big dogs fighting for Tampa... Let's just focus and become the king of Brandon." We concentrated all our advertising on the east side of I-75 and the south side of I-4. Those were our parameters: Brandon, Plant City, Riverview, Ruskin, Valrico, and Fish Hawk. It's a huge area, of course, but even to this day, our four billboards are all in that area.

We applied the same approach to our commercials. Although Bay News 9 / Spectrum has three geographic locations, we stayed in the east zone, focusing on our designated area.

Now, of course, we've expanded, and we do cases all over Florida. We even have clients in other states. It really is crazy if you think about it.

(In 2015, Ryan and I tried a slip and fall case in Orlando. Lee-Ann was still in high school, so we couldn't stay overnight. We had to leave Brandon at 6:00 in the morning, try the case, drive back, and head back out the next morning—we did this for four days. In case you were wondering, I-4 was just as bad then as it is now. It is still called Die 4!)

So we do handle cases in other parts of Florida and elsewhere, but Brandon—our hometown—is the heart of our business, and the majority of our clientele is still in that geographic area. We grew our business by focusing on serving the community we live in, where we grew up, helping our neighbors and friends. And that's the way we plan to keep it.

Our First Official Employee

Roy's wife, Michelle, was working at a downtown Tampa personal injury firm as a paralegal when we started Reed & Reed. Michelle desperately wanted to work for us, but we simply did not have the money to hire her. She's my best friend's wife, and she is arguably the most knowledgeable personal injury paralegal in the business. I wanted to offer her a job, but that did not change the fact we were still broke. She kept asking, "When can I put in my two-week notice and come to work for Reed & Reed?" but I kept telling her, "We have no money! You've gotta hang in there."

At this point, Ryan and I weren't even taking paychecks. We

182 ———————————————————————— PAUL REED

took enough money from the account each month to pay the bills for home and work. If we did something extra, it came from the money Jackie made playing poker at the casino. Believe it or not, those were good times!

Well, on Monday, January 6, 2014—just a few months after Reed & Reed started—Michelle showed up to work at the Tampa law firm with a hangover. The office manager started nagging and griping at her, and Michelle just said, "Screw this, I quit." She walked out, hangover and all.

So I got the call the next day: "Oh, by the way, I start with Reed & Reed tomorrow."

I said, "Michelle, I don't have money. How am I going to pay you?"

But we figured out a way, and Michelle came onboard—at just $12 per hour at first, a significant reduction in pay. I'm actually glad she joined when she did, because Ryan and I had just invested in a software called Needles. It was (and still is) the best program out there for managing client data, case files, and paperwork for injury law firms, but it was also the most expensive. At the time, it cost approximately six or seven thousand dollars. This was a huge investment, but I told Ryan, "We gotta bite the bullet and get it." When the program was installed, there was not one piece of information in the system. It took several weeks to input the client information for the fifty or so clients we had. Luckily, Ryan and I had plenty of time on our hands back then. I look at how many files we have in the system now, the documents Michelle has created over the years, the closed/settled cases... It still amazes me how much we have grown. We are truly blessed!

The Third Reed

Jackie (Jacquelyn) became the third lawyer here at Reed & Reed. She's Ryan's wife, and my daughter-in-law... she's the third Reed. But as I said earlier, she didn't work with us right away. We couldn't afford to pay her!

Soon after we started Reed & Reed, Jackie's job search led her to a competing firm in Tampa. (Jackie was getting a lot of quality experience on someone else's dime, but she wanted to join the "family," so to speak.)

I just kept telling her, "Hang in there. You need the experience, and we can't afford to hire you right now... just hang in there."

In December of 2016, we finally had enough money to hire Jackie, and the rest is history! The three of us have been "kickin' %@#" ever since.

It's hard to explain the blessing it is to work with my family—there's truly nothing like it. Together, we're building a legacy.

A Place of Our Own

In January of 2017, a local attorney was selling his office building. He advertised it, with a little sign outside, as "the oldest law firm in Brandon." He'd been around for a long time, and was retiring and downsizing. We got word he was selling it, and we could finally afford our own place, so we bought it.

The building also happens to be on a corner lot, directly on the Fourth of July parade route for Brandon. In the years pre-COVID, we hosted annual parties for our friends and clients and their families. We provided delicious barbecue catered from a local restaurant, water slides, drinks, and desserts, and anyone who wanted to could come early to watch the parade. Fun, family, and community—it's how we do things.

Sadly, they canceled the parade in 2020, 2021, and 2022.

But the fact that we now conduct business out of an office that was once the oldest law firm in Brandon is pretty cool, too.

Saying Goodbye to Keith

My brother Keith died on December 17, 2017—a Sunday—just a couple days after the Reed & Reed annual Christmas party.

We had the Christmas party at the Hard Rock on Friday, December 15th, and Keith came. He had his fanny pack of drugs on him... marijuana, Xanax, oxi... by that point, his body was used to that crap. That, and alcohol. All downers. But a few months earlier, come to find out, Keith started using cocaine again.

Ricky Margison had been living with Keith at 108 Rosier for probably ten years by that point, maybe more. He said about six weeks before Keith died, he started becoming really paranoid (cocaine makes some people react that way; it's a stimulant). Ricky said on two occasions, Keith thought the cops were outside his house. He freaked out, ran out the back door, jumped the fence, all that—and no one was even there. Ricky had told him, "You need to quit snorting that @#$%!"

But of course, Keith didn't listen.

Anyway, at the Christmas party, Keith just started pulling out all his drugs from his fanny pack, and putting them on the bar. I had to make him put it away. I was like, "Come on, man. You can't put that out on the counter."

But Keith thought it was cool.

Anyway, the party ended, and Keith went home.

Ricky said that on Saturday, Keith was fine. About 1 p.m. or 2 p.m. they ate, and watched TV.

On Sunday, around 11 a.m., Ricky got up, and Keith still wasn't up. Keith was an early riser, so Ricky went to check on him.

Keith's room was barricaded. He had apparently gotten all paranoid and put something up against the door.

When Keith didn't answer, Ricky busted in... and Keith was in bed, dead, clutching a big knife.

I was in church that morning, and I don't take my phone into church—I always check my messages right after, but church is the one hour per week that I don't keep my phone on me. I've always thought people shouldn't; if you can't go one hour without it... but that's another topic. Anyway, I came out to my car, and I saw a message: *Call Keith's house. Urgent.*

I thought, "What did he do now?" So I called.

Ricky answered, and I could tell something was up, so I asked, "What's going on?"

Ricky simply said, "Keith's dead."

I was in shock, obviously, but I said, "Huh. How'd he die?" The choices in my mind were car wreck, fight, or drugs.

Ricky said, "I'm assuming he overdosed on something."

CHAPTER
TEN

So I said, "That's messed up. Okay..." I mean, in times like that, you're numb. Then I asked, "Have you told anybody else?"

Ricky said, "No. I figured you would."

So I called Jody: "Ain't no easy way to say this... Keith's dead."

There are some things you won't forget. Even though half the time I can't remember my kids' names, I remember this conversation perfectly—Jody said, "Huh. How'd he die?"

I told him, "Evidently, he overdosed last night."

"Oh... Did you tell Mom?"

I said, "You're the older brother! You're supposed to tell Mom!"

Jody said, "I ain't telling her."

So I ended up having to call Mom. And that was brutal.

Then I had to call Keith's daughter to tell her, and that was brutal, too.

It's sad... Keith did not have to die like that. I do not condone doing drugs, but if you do, there comes a time when you need to "hang up your cleats." The statistics show that an average of 192 people died *daily* in 2017 from a drug overdose, and Keith had just become one of them.

The next person I called was Brian, his lifelong friend. I said, "Keith's dead."

He asked, "How'd he die?"

"How do you think?"

Brian said, "Car crash, someone killed him, or drugs."

I said, "It was drugs."

"Oh. Okay."

It wasn't a shocker that Keith was gonna die young; the over-under was thirty years old. He blew by that and hit fifty, but it was still sad. He didn't have to die that way. I'll probably punch him in the face the next time I see him, for being stupid... then give him a big hug.

See you soon enough, Moreeder.

Chapter 11

◆—○————————————○—◆

More Hairballs

This chapter contains some of Michelle's favorite hairballs from the years since I started Reed & Reed—or at least *my* favorite hairballs. (Michelle is probably glaring at me from somewhere, right now.) The hairballs in this chapter are some of the ones that got *interesting*, in one way or another. These cases include criminal appeals, business issues, disability rights, parental rights, and more. Some of these cases spiraled out of control, some were a blast to work, while others were just funny. In any case, I think you'll find them entertaining, and possibly even enlightening. With pro bono "hairball" cases, there's almost always something interesting to learn.

The Other Side of Twiggs Street

The client in this case was a Brandon boy; I grew up with him. I don't do criminal law, but this case did not require a criminal law attorney because, in all honesty, my friend had no defense. He was on DUI probation when he was involved in *another* DUI, and fled the scene. When the cops came knocking, he let them in and confessed everything. My friend was an alcoholic who needed help and treatment, but if you violate probation, you don't get to bond out. You have to go before the violation of probation judge—and that may not be the next day, or even the next week. In the meantime, my friend went to jail. He needed a lawyer to negotiate the best outcome for him moving forward, so I stepped in to help him.

I called my buddy who does criminal law, and asked him, "Hey, what do I need to do?"

He told me I needed to get a hearing date to address the violation. So I did. We got assigned to this one judge who was a good man and a fair judge, but also scary. (I don't think being a "nice guy" judge plays very well in violation of probation court.)

I am also friends with a state attorney who has worked in the criminal justice arena for twenty years. I called him and he told me, "Just don't B.S. this judge."

I was like, "No B.S. Got it."

On the day of the probation hearing, the courtroom was full of lawyers

How I Do Criminal Court

I'm like a fish out of water when I walk into criminal court. I have no idea what the heck I'm doing—so I go in and wing it. I stand up: "Your honor, this is not my area of expertise... I've never done this before..."

When you walk into the criminal courts, you are just one out of a big stack of cases. You walk in, they grab your file, and they're like (for example), "Okay, we got Crystal, she got caught with marijuana, first offense... we'll do withhold adjudication, court costs and a $500 fine."

And the judge says, "Okay. Next!"

So, all I can do in those cases is walk up and say, "This is a friend of mine. This is what they're charged with. What can you do to help them?"

As long as you aren't being rude, the judge might be willing to work with you. If the client got caught smoking pot or something, there's not much of a defense for that. So I play stupid. "It's a nice person over there, they did whatever; what can you do for them?" That's how I do criminal court.

and probation officers scattered throughout the room. I was sitting in the juror's section, because it had padded seats that were more comfortable. Some of the lawyers and probation officers were in there with me, while others sat in the pews. The judge was up in the podium. Over to the side were the bailiffs and the convicts in their orange jumpsuits, all handcuffed and chained together.

In these types of hearings, they call the Defendants' names one at a time, and the lawyer goes up to speak for them, or if they don't have a lawyer, the Defendant gets up to talk to the judge. Then the judge explains what he's gonna do. He can send the Defendant to jail, or add additional time to the probation, or he can say, "Okay, don't do it again; continue on with your original probation"—he can do all kinds of things.

While that process was going on, I was talking to a lady sitting near me. I don't recall if she was a probation officer, or if she was with DACCO, a drug and alcohol treatment program. (The reality is, most of these probation violations are drug or alcohol related.)

She told me, "Well, you basically have three options. The judge can send your client to prison, he can give your client inpatient treatment for six to eighteen months, or he can put what's called a SCRAM bracelet on your client and let him have out-patient treatment for his alcohol issues—the SCRAM bracelet detects alcohol." (Seriously, if you even shampoo with a product that has alcohol in it, the SCRAM is gonna go off and the cops are gonna pick you up for violating the conditions of your release; it's that sensitive.)

I was like, *Well, alright. What do I have to lose? Let's ask for the SCRAM plan.* I knew my client wouldn't want to go to jail, and he probably didn't want to go to a treatment program, even though it would've helped him. The SCRAM bracelet was probably his best bet.

While we were waiting for our turn, the judge called a female prisoner. She was in her mid-to-late twenties. She stood up in her chains and jumpsuit, and the judge had her confirm her name, then he read off the charge. She had violated on a drug issue, some kind of theft related to drugs.

The judge asked her, "Where do you get your drugs?"
She said, "I don't know."
He said, "What do you mean, you don't know?"
She said, "Some guy."

CHAPTER
ELEVEN

The judge said, "So you just get your drugs from *some guy?* What do you do, just walk up to the convenience store and go up to *some guy* and say, 'Hey, got any drugs?'"

The girl said, "No. I know him through a friend."

"But you don't know his name?"

"No."

"Do you know where he lives?"

"No."

By this point, the judge was getting frustrated. The girl was rolling her eyes, using a sarcastic tone, making faces—just being really disrespectful.

She had a lawyer with her. I don't think he was a public defender; he was just this guy in a cheap suit, weighing maybe 120 pounds, standing up there, not saying a word.

Now, in these situations, you only speak when spoken to. Especially with this judge, you didn't speak out of turn. He would let you know when he was speaking to the Defendant, or when he had a question for the lawyer, and you didn't talk unless he was talking to you and asked for a response. So this guy was just standing there as the judge asked the Defendant a few more questions, and she just kept giving the judge that sarcastic attitude.

Finally, the judge got angry. He flipped through his papers. "You know what I'm gonna do?" *Bam!* He hit the gavel on the podium. "Ten years in prison. Goodbye!"

The girl started *freaking* out, screaming and everything.

The lawyer yelled, "Your honor! Your honor!"

The judge said, "Counselor, another word out of you and you'll be going with her!"

That lawyer turned around, gave his client the salute, and booked it out of there.

Then the bailiffs scooped up the girl, and out the door *she* went, too.

So now, the mood in the courtroom turned "south," so to speak. The judge was irritated, which was the last thing anyone wanted. You can also imagine what every lawyer in the room dreaded after something like that: to be the next one called.

Thank God, we weren't next, but he called up this young teenager, small in stature, probably eighteen or nineteen years old. He called out the prisoner's case number and name.

That kid popped right up: "Your honor, I get my drugs from Bobby Mac! I'll tell the bailiff, I'll show you where he's at. We can go *right now!*"

The judge started laughing, everyone was laughing, and the judge said, "Well, I appreciate your enthusiasm, but just hold up a second. Let's go over your case."

The judge worked his way through that case and we moved on, but it was pretty darn funny and it broke the tension.

At some point in time, my client's case was called. I went up to the stand.

I'd met the judge a couple times before; he was a fisherman. I like to fish. (Reed & Reed actually has a fishing commercial) So we had something in common. Although I didn't know the judge very well, he knew who I was.

He said, "Mr. Reed! I don't usually see you on this side of the street." (The criminal court is on one side of Twiggs Street in downtown Tampa, and the civil court is on the other.)

I said, "No, sir. I'm like a fish out of water here, but I grew up with my client. And there's no real defense, but I played baseball with"—and I named my state attorney friend. (If you don't think I name drop in the criminal justice system, then "You've got another thing comin'," quoting Judas Priest.)

The judge said, "Oh, I know him well."

I said, "Well, he told me, just don't B.S. you."

The judge said, "That's good advice. All of the rest of you should listen to that advice."

So I said, "Here's where we're at. My client was on probation for DUI. He's now back in front of you, sitting over there."

My client stood up, still in his chains. Now, he was also a small guy, bald-headed with a little goatee—he kind of looked like a smaller, thinner version of Walter White from *Breaking Bad.* And he was *shaking*, literally.

I said, "Your honor, my client is an alcoholic. He's got a serious problem."

The judge asked my client, "Mr. X, Do you agree with your lawyer?"

"Yes, sir."

The judge said, "Well, Mr. Reed, what are we gonna *do* with Mr. X?"

I said, "Well, your honor, again, this is not my area at all. But I was talking to that young lady over there, and she said there are three options."

The judge said, "Well, okay. I know her well. I hope she gave you sound advice."

I said, "Well, we'll know soon enough."

Judge kind of laughed, then he said, "Well, what did she tell you?"

I said, "Option one: my client goes to jail."

The judge turned to my client. "You like option number one?"

"No, sir."

"I wouldn't either! Okay, Mr. Reed, back to you. What's option number two?"

I said, "My client goes to an inpatient drug and alcohol treatment program."

The judge said, "Okay, that's an option. What's option number three?"

I said, "Well, your honor, it's my understanding there's this device called a SCRAM bracelet that monitors your alcohol intake. She said what happens is you put the device on my client, and he goes to *outpatient* treatment. If my client drinks or violates, then we would be back here, and I'm sure my client would be on his way to one of the finer institutions in the state of Florida."

The judge said, "Well, okay!" He turned to my client. "Mr. X, I'm not going to put you in jail. But you have two choices. I do believe, and take your word for it, that you are an alcoholic. It's admirable that you've admitted to that. So would you like to go to an inpatient treatment facility, or—I understand you have a job—we could put a SCRAM bracelet on you. If we do that, I want to tell you: if you violate the probation, I'm giving you three years in prison. What do you want to do?"

My client said, "Your honor, I've learned my lesson, and I want to keep my job. I'll take the SCRAM bracelet with the understanding that if I violate, I'm going to three years in prison."

So that's what happened, and my client successfully completed his probation.

After he completed probation, he invited my whole family to his parents' lake house for a weekend, as a thank you for helping him.

His parents had a very nice two-story lake house, with a boat and all that. The first night we were there, we were out on the boat on this huge lake, and there was a section just *littered* with alligators. As for my friend/client, that six-month sobriety didn't stick long, for him. He was hammered, and he was driving the boat. He started hauling butt, doing turns—it really wasn't funny, because if we got flipped out, there were alligators everywhere. That was Friday night.

Saturday, we swam and skied (in a different part of the lake), and later that night had a barbecue. That was a good day. We were leaving the next day, Sunday.

My bed was near the kitchen, and around 5:30 or 6:00 a.m. on Sunday, I heard him in the kitchen. Come to find out, he was taking shots of booze. (He didn't want his parents to know he started drinking again, so he was taking shots out of several different bottles so his parents would not know the booze was gone.) By the time we got up to get ready to leave around 10 a.m., he was passed out in a lawn chair down by the lake. We didn't even get to say goodbye.

I didn't hear from him again—the next I heard, he had passed away. One word: "Sad."

The Not-Stolen Car

The client in this case was a friend I've known for more than thirty years. He's a Brandon boy, a redneck through and through. His wife had a drug problem, allegedly. At the time this all happened, their relationship was strained—basically, they'd been married forever, so they stuck together, but they argued a lot and seemed like they couldn't stand each other half the time. Definitely a love-hate relationship. My friend was working for the Hillsborough County Sheriff's department as a guard at the jail in Brandon. My friend's wife was interacting with police on the *other* side of things.

This particular evening, my buddy's wife "befriended" a boy in the neighborhood who was in his late teens to early twenties, and invited him over to "hang out."

My friend went to bed.

Evidently, at some point in the night, the party supplies ran out. Here is where the story veers left and right, depending on whom you ask.

The boy said that when the "supplies" ran out, he was given the keys to her car so he could go buy more.

On his way back to the house, the boy was speeding, weaving in and out of traffic, and he hit and killed a woman. (She was married, and the mother of two young kids). The crash happened early the next morning, 4 to 5 a.m.

That morning, my friend was woken up by someone banging on his front door.

As my friend entered the living room, he saw his wife asleep on the couch—and when he opened the door there were two police officers standing there.

"What's going on?" my friend asked one of the officers.

The officer replied, "Your car was involved in a fatal crash."

My friend was like, "What are you talking about?" My friend told his wife, "Wake up! The cops are here, and our car was involved in a fatal crash last night!"

His wife's story was, "The boy must've taken my keys while I was asleep and stolen the car. I don't know anything more than that."

The boy was in the hospital—it was a head-on collision, a bad crash—and he was saying, "No, she gave me the keys. I didn't steal the car."

Now, as the owner of the car, my friend was responsible for that woman's death—not criminally, but civilly. Under the dangerous instrumentality doctrine, the driver is responsible, and so is the vehicle's owner.

My friend had $10,000 in bodily injury liability coverage on his auto insurance policy, which is not much, needless to say, for a fatal car crash situation.

The cops were investigating to determine whether they would charge the kid with theft of the car, which could possibly lead to a felony murder charge: "You stole a car, and in the course of that theft, you killed somebody."

As I said, the husband was a friend, so I agreed to help him. This was a personal injury case, but my friend was the Defendant, not the injured Plaintiff. I only represented him, not his wife. Given what the boy in the hospital was saying, the police did not believe his wife's version of events. I am not sure anyone believed her. Regardless, I told my friend/client that his wife would have to get her own lawyer.

As the case worked its way through the system, detectives interviewed my client. His part was simple: "The kid lives in the neighborhood. I've seen him around but I don't really know him. He came over, and I went to bed. Next thing I knew, I was waking up to the cops at the door."

Jumping ahead, nobody was ever charged criminally for the crash. But, my client, his wife, and the kid driving the car were all sued by the deceased woman's estate. The insurance company my client had for auto insurance was notorious as one of the *worst* insurance companies to deal with when it comes to personal injury... and they weren't wanting to pay out the $10,000. The woman's husband had a lawyer, and they wanted compensation (rightfully!) for her death. But my client's insurance company took the position that even though it was my client's car, since it was "stolen," my client wasn't responsible.

Now, if someone actually steals your car, you're not responsible for what happens while they are driving it, even as the car's owner. There are exceptions to this general rule, if you leave the keys accessible. Example #1: You leave your keys in the car when you run into the convenience store and the car is stolen. From a civil liability perspective, you can still be held liable for any injuries caused by the thief while driving your car. Example #2: You leave your keys lying on the counter and one of your kid's friends takes the keys and the car without permission; you can still be held liable for any injuries caused by the kid while driving your car.

In this case, the kid *did* have the keys—yet the insurance company was taking the position that the car was still stolen, so they weren't responsible to pay.

This was one of the dumbest positions an insurance company

has ever taken, at least one that I have seen. They should have hand-delivered the $10,000 to that woman's husband immediately! In fact, as my client's insurance company, they had a duty to protect the insured. They should have *run* that money over to the husband in exchange for a release of claim. This could have prevented the lawsuit eventually filed by the deceased woman's estate. But they didn't.

So my client got sued as the owner of the vehicle. My client was on the hook, now, for *millions* of dollars. (Remember, the deceased was a wife and mother of young children.)

I represented my client, but there was really nothing my client could say or do. He was asleep when it happened, he didn't give the guy the keys; he really had nothing to do with this process other than owning the car. Unfortunately, he was simply getting dragged along in this tragic mess.

My client's wife was sticking to her story. At this point, she had no choice. Providing false information to an insurance company is a felony punishable by up to five years in prison. This course of action only fostered the insurance company's position that it didn't have to pay.

As the case progressed with interrogatories, depositions, non-party production, motions, etc., the lawyers representing the Plaintiff (i.e., the deceased woman's estate) hired a "big dog" out of Miami who specialized in bad faith litigation. Insurance companies have a duty to protect their clients from an excess judgment— meaning, as I said, my client's insurance company should've *run* that $10,000 to the husband and said, "We're going to tender the policy limits." The husband wouldn't have settled for such a small amount, but from an insurance perspective, my client's insurance company had a duty to *try* to protect its client by tendering the limits and getting him a release.

Instead, my client's insurance company rode the "stolen vehicle" theory like a Texas cowboy rides a bull! So the bad faith position being argued by the Miami lawyer was simple: "The insurance company should've attempted to tender (pay) the $10,000 policy limits. It should have known the law worked against my client, i.e., the kid had access to the keys even if my client's wife did not give him permission to drive the car. It should have viewed my client's wife's statement with skepticism since the kid said he was given the keys on the night of the crash. And now, the insurance company has hung my client out to dry and left him possibly on the hook for millions of dollars. That's bad faith." So they were going after the insurance company from that angle. Game on.

After a year or so of pre-trial discovery, the case was mediated. Mediation is basically an attempt to settle the case before trial. It was Friday, so I strolled in wearing a pair of jeans and a Reed & Reed shirt with my client—and I swear, you'd have thought you were at a Wall Street stock brokers' meeting. There were walls of TV screens, and people in thousand-dollar suits and Rolex watches— lawyers and insurance personnel everywhere.

The table was full, so I just said, "We'll sit in the back of the room here and watch." There was really nothing my client or I could say or do at this point, anyway.

The Miami lawyer went on for an hour on bad faith, explaining what the insurance company did wrong, how many judgments for millions and millions of dollars he'd gotten from insurance companies, how they had screwed up and were gonna pay, etc. Of course, then the insurance company's lawyers got up and gave their side—blah, blah, blah. Then they started bouncing numbers back and forth.

At lunch time, I told my client, "We don't need to be here. We've seen what we need to see, and there's nothing more we can do right now." I turned to the hometown lawyer for the insurance company, and said, "We're gonna go. Just update us if they reach a settlement."

Well, the case settled. There was a confidentiality agreement in the release so I cannot divulge the settlement amount. That having been said, "Bing, bang, boing!" My client got his release—he was off the hook. But the insurance company should have offered its policy limits to settle the case from the very beginning.

This is a tragic story—I'm truly sorry for that woman's death, and for her family's loss. But it's also a cautionary tale about how insurance companies work. They will often find *any* reason they can to avoid paying out (especially certain insurance companies). You cannot just assume that they'll pay out what they should, even if you have that coverage on your policy. If that insurance company had not been held accountable for its duty to its client, things could have turned out very differently.

The Party in Clearwater

The guy in this situation was one of Ryan's friends, just a great, lovable, teddy-bear kind of guy. He had called me a few times before for help. For example, once he got in a tussle with the gate at his housing complex. The sign said *One vehicle at a time*, but he tried to skirt through the gate behind another car, and it ripped the back bumper off his BMW.

He called me, and I was like, "Did it say one at a time?"

"Well, yeah, but normally you can get through!"

"Well, normally," I said. "But there's nothing I can do for you."

Anyway, this other time, I got a call at 2 a.m.

Normally, at two in the morning, people are calling because there's something wrong. No one calls in the middle of the night just to see if you're awake. So when people call late, I still answer, because you never know—like with Roy's story.

Anyway, I saw it was Ryan's friend, so I answered the phone. "What's up?"

(This is probably a good time to add that this guy and his friends were in college at the time—they were under twenty-one.)

Ryan's friend, in panic mode, said, "I'm at my grandmother's condo in Clearwater having a little party, and the cops just walked in the back sliding glass door."

"It wasn't locked?" I asked.

"No, people may have been going in and out."

"Was it shut?"

"Yeah."

"Did anybody invite them in?"

"No. They knocked on the front door. We saw them out the peephole and got quiet, then they just walked around the back and came in."

I said, "Okay."

Then I heard the cop in the background: "Who you talking to? Get off the phone!"

The guy said, "I'm talking to my lawyer."

The cop said, all snarky, "Oh, you've got a lawyer on speed dial?"

The guy said, "Well, yeah, it's my buddy's dad who's a lawyer."

The cop said, "Let me talk to this so-called lawyer."

So the guy handed the cop the phone.

"Who's this?" the cop asked.

"Paul Reed."

"You a lawyer?"

"Yeah."

The cop said, "You let kids call you all hours of the night?"

"Well, I'm not happy about it," I said, "but he evidently is in a situation that requires legal advice, and he's my son's best friend—but forget all that. Now that I have you on the phone, what are you doing?"

The cop said, "What do you mean? We got a noise complaint."

I said, "Well, I understand that. And you knocked on the front door, correct?"

"Yeah, and they didn't answer," the cop said.

"Okay... so then you went around back on private property, and let yourself into his condominium without a warrant... How do you think that's going to play out in court? You think that's going to go well for you?"

"Uhhh..."

I said, "Do me a favor so I can go back to bed, do yourself a favor so I don't have to embarrass you later in court, and more importantly, do the state attorney and judge a favor—harass the kids, pour their crap out, I don't care, but don't arrest them. Because that's not going to go well for you."

I heard a noise, then silence... Come to find out, the cop threw the guy's phone and smashed it against the wall. But he did what I said: he harassed them, did whatever he did, and left without arresting anybody.

Ryan's friend called me a couple days later—he reminds me of Keith, to be honest— and said, "I want to sue the cop! He owes me a thousand dollars for the phone he broke!"

So I said, "Well, count that as your attorney's fee for waking me up, so you and the cop are even. You just threw a $1000 party."

All's well that ends well!

(If anyone is ever vacationing from out of state, here's a word of advice: Clearwater Police DO NOT PLAY! Mind your P's and Q's, especially with alcohol, or you may find yourself staying the night in the Hotel De Slaughter—that means jail.)

The Lottery Ticket

For purposes of this story, I am going to use the terms *Plaintiff* and *Defendant*, rather than names.

The story begins on April 25, 2017, but first, a little background information. The Defendant was living in a mobile home with his girlfriend and their two children. The Plaintiff, a male friend of the Defendant, was living in the back part of the trailer. The Plaintiff was admittedly addicted to methamphetamine, a self-described "meth head." The Plaintiff was homeless when he met the Defendant in January 2017. The Defendant, feeling sorry for the Plaintiff, began giving him odd jobs to do around the house: taking care of the yard, the house, the dogs, etc. At some point during the budding friendship, the Defendant saw the Plaintiff bathing in the hose. Seeing this, the Defendant asked the Plaintiff if he would like to move in with him (and the family). Of course, the invitation was accepted.

The night of April 25th is where the stories begin to diverge.

The Plaintiff claimed that late in the afternoon, the Defendant "paid" him for services rendered around the property with $40 worth of meth. The Plaintiff then went over to a friend's house and sold $20 worth of that meth. Next, the Plaintiff used the $20 to purchase two $10 scratch-off lottery tickets. According to the Plaintiff, after purchasing the tickets, he did some "dumpster diving" before returning home. The Plaintiff alleged he returned home at approximately 4:30 a.m., then scratched off the ticket. The ticket was a million dollar winner. The Plaintiff was so high on meth he thought the ticket was a $100,000.00 winner. When the Plaintiff arrived at the homestead early that morning, he caused the dogs to bark, which woke up the Defendant. The Defendant came into the living room to find out what was going on. The Plaintiff told him that he (the Plaintiff) had won $100,000. The Plaintiff showed the Defendant the ticket, and the Defendant confirmed the winning ticket: "Yes, it's a winner for $100,000."

(In fact, it was a $1 million dollar winning ticket. You can't make this stuff up, right?)

Anyway, the Plaintiff, thinking he won $100,000, offered to pay the Defendant $10,000 to take the ticket to Tallahassee and cash it for him. The government would take 25 percent, the Defendant would get his $10,000, and the Plaintiff would get the rest ($65,000).

Needless to say, the Defendant's version of events differs from the Plaintiff's version. The Defendant's version of the April 25-26 events goes like this:

The Defendant claims he gave the Plaintiff $30 for two purposes: to go buy the Defendant two scratch-off lottery tickets, and to get himself, the Plaintiff, some cigarettes. The Defendant did not see or hear from the Plaintiff until he returned home around 4:30 a.m. The barking dogs woke the Defendant up. The Plaintiff gave the Defendant the two lottery tickets and went back outside to quiet the barking dogs. The Defendant, who typically got up at 5 a.m. to go to work, put on a pot of coffee and scratched off the tickets—winning one million dollars. He woke up his girlfriend, made arrangements for the grandma to watch the children, and went to Tallahassee to cash in the ticket.

This whole case hinges on one point: If I give you $20 to go buy me beer, that's not your beer, right? The lottery ticket is no different. If I gave you money to go buy me something, it doesn't become yours just because you were the one who physically went to the store and purchased it. So the legal question is simple: did the Plaintiff use his own money to buy the tickets, or did he use the Defendant's money to buy the tickets for the Defendant?

But that's not all that happened here, so let's keep going...

The Defendant went to Tallahassee to cash the ticket on his behalf, as I mentioned earlier. Once the Defendant returned from

Tallahassee, the Plaintiff said he asked the Defendant for the $65,000 from his winnings.

The Defendant told the Plaintiff it would take a few days for the money to be placed into the Defendant's account.

The Plaintiff claimed he was then given $1000 to "hold him over." (Remember, meth is involved in this case.)

The Defendant, on the other hand, said he gave the Plaintiff money, but that it was more than $1,000: the Defendant claimed the Plaintiff had legal issues that needed financial attention, and that he (the Defendant) was simply helping his friend.

We have to do some math on this one, because the amount of money allegedly given to the Plaintiff by the Defendant is crucial to both the Plaintiff's case and Defendant's case.

The Plaintiff also claimed that a few days later, he was given $35,000 more dollars (making the total to date $36,000) of the $65,000.

The Defendant says he never gave the Plaintiff $35,000.

At some point in time, shortly after receiving the $35,000, the Plaintiff made his way to his criminal defense attorney's office. I assume it was to pay the attorney for criminal services rendered on an unrelated matter. The Plaintiff was carrying the money around in a backpack. Yep, a backpack. At some point during the meeting with his criminal defense attorney, the Plaintiff said, "Hey, I won $100,000!" and showed him the money in his backpack. A lot of other things transpired with the Plaintiff, the attorney, and the $35,000, but that would make a two-hour movie, or book all by itself! Anyway, at this point in the story, the Defendant had allegedly given the Plaintiff $36,000 of the agreed-upon $65,000.

Around this time, the Defendant decided it was time for the Plaintiff to find another place to live. Each party's version of events differs again at this point.

The Defendant claims that he planned to give his friend money to get a vehicle and a place to live.

The Plaintiff claims he was getting "kicked out" because the Defendant did not want him (the Plaintiff) to know the ticket was a million dollar winner. (From the Plaintiff's perspective, it would have been difficult for the Defendant to spend all that money under his nose.)

After a few more weeks, the Plaintiff moved out, but he was angry about it. After all, he had given the Defendant $10,000 to cash in the winning lottery ticket, and had now been kicked out. The saga continues.

In the Plaintiff's version of events, he was still owed $29,00.00. The relationship had gone south by now. Accordingly, the Defendant did not give the Plaintiff any more money. The Plaintiff and Defendant communicated via text messages at this point.

(Public service announcement: although somewhat gibberish, the texts did not support the Defendant's position. Be careful what you text.)

So what did the Plaintiff do? He reached out to his criminal defense attorney for help. The attorney allegedly read the text message and came to the conclusion that his client, the Plaintiff, was still owed $29,000. So the attorney called the Defendant and demanded payment in the amount of $29,000.

Initially, the Defendant denied owing the Plaintiff any money. I mean, the ticket belonged to the Defendant, right? But there were those text messages.

The attorney said to the Defendant, "I read the text message." The Defendant allegedly responded, "Oh, you did?"

Shortly thereafter, $29,000 was wired into the Plaintiff's bank account. However, it was the Defendant's position that he did not owe the Plaintiff any money, but gave him the money to get the attorney "off his back," and because the Defendant and Plaintiff had been friends at one time.

(I cannot say it enough: meth was a factor in all decision making at this time. The Defendant just wanted the Plaintiff to leave him alone.)

End of the story, right? Nope! The Defendant started spending his winnings: cars, clothes, new house, etc., at which point the Plaintiff's girlfriend got suspicious. Where was all this money coming from? $10,000 does not buy all of the things being purchased by the Defendant.

So what did the girlfriend do? She went to the Florida Lottery website and discovered the ticket was a million dollar winner. (Unlike other states, Florida Lottery ticket winners are not confidential.)

Boom! As you can imagine, the Plaintiff made a beeline to his attorney's office.

Being a criminal defense attorney, the first thing the Plaintiff's attorney did was call the police to report a crime: fraud and theft. Next, as a former prosecutor, he called one of his old buddies on the police force and asked the detective to investigate the case.

Again, there was so much more that occurred, but that is fodder for another day.

The detective investigated the case. He did not find any evidence that supported the Plaintiff's position that the ticket belonged to him. No criminal charges were ever filed. Dead end.

So what does any good lawyer do at this point? Yep, file a civil lawsuit against the Defendant. The criminal attorney filed an ex parte motion to freeze any money still in the Defendant's bank account. However, by the time this happened, there was a little less than $10,000 remaining in the account.

You can see the full scope of what the Plaintiff was claiming in the Amended Complaint included in the next couple pages. (Basically, it shows the Plaintiff's position on exactly what I've explained so far. These documents are all public record, but for the purposes of this book, I've redacted the names and identifying info.)

IN THE CIRCUIT COURT OF THE ███████ JUDICIAL CIRCUIT
IN AND FOR ████████████████

████████████████,

    Plaintiff,   CASE NO.: ████████████

vs.

████████████ ████████████,
And ████████████████,
A Foreign Corporation,
    Defendants.

_____/

FIRST AMENDED COMPLAINT

    Plaintiff ████████████████ sues defendants ████████████ ████████████████ and states as follows:

1.   This is an action that exceeds $30,000.00, exclusive of costs, fees, and interest.

2.   All material facts occurred in ████████ Florida.

3.   All parties are residents of ████████ Florida.

4.   This Court has jurisdiction over the parties and causes of action.

5.   ████████ is the proper venue for this lawsuit.

6.   All conditions precedent to the filing of this lawsuit have occurred or have been waived by Defendant.

7.   On or about April 24 or 25, 2017, ████████ purchased a Florida lottery scratch-off ticket (hereinafter "the ticket") in ████████ Florida.

8.   ████████ scratched off the ticket and believed he had won a prize of $100,000.00.

9.   ████████ showed the ticket to ████████ on April 25, 2017.

10.   ████████ told ████████ the ticket was a $100,000.00 winning ticket.

11.   ████████, who had no driver's license nor other form of official identification, asked ████████ if ████████ would redeem the ticket for ████████ at the Florida lottery offices.

12.   ████████ agreed to redeem the ticket for a fee of $10,000.00, which

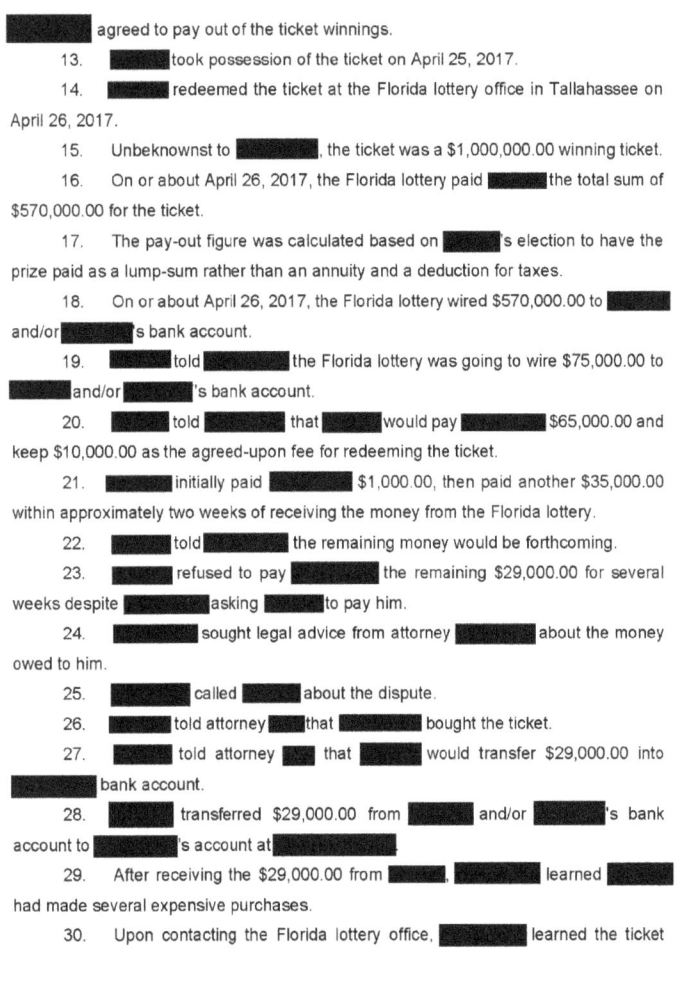

agreed to pay out of the ticket winnings.

13. ▉▉▉ took possession of the ticket on April 25, 2017.

14. ▉▉▉ redeemed the ticket at the Florida lottery office in Tallahassee on April 26, 2017.

15. Unbeknownst to ▉▉▉, the ticket was a $1,000,000.00 winning ticket.

16. On or about April 26, 2017, the Florida lottery paid ▉▉▉ the total sum of $570,000.00 for the ticket.

17. The pay-out figure was calculated based on ▉▉▉'s election to have the prize paid as a lump-sum rather than an annuity and a deduction for taxes.

18. On or about April 26, 2017, the Florida lottery wired $570,000.00 to ▉▉▉ and/or ▉▉▉'s bank account.

19. ▉▉▉ told ▉▉▉ the Florida lottery was going to wire $75,000.00 to ▉▉▉ and/or ▉▉▉'s bank account.

20. ▉▉▉ told ▉▉▉ that ▉▉▉ would pay ▉▉▉ $65,000.00 and keep $10,000.00 as the agreed-upon fee for redeeming the ticket.

21. ▉▉▉ initially paid ▉▉▉ $1,000.00, then paid another $35,000.00 within approximately two weeks of receiving the money from the Florida lottery.

22. ▉▉▉ told ▉▉▉ the remaining money would be forthcoming.

23. ▉▉▉ refused to pay ▉▉▉ the remaining $29,000.00 for several weeks despite ▉▉▉ asking ▉▉▉ to pay him.

24. ▉▉▉ sought legal advice from attorney ▉▉▉ about the money owed to him.

25. ▉▉▉ called ▉▉▉ about the dispute.

26. ▉▉▉ told attorney ▉▉▉ that ▉▉▉ bought the ticket.

27. ▉▉▉ told attorney ▉▉▉ that ▉▉▉ would transfer $29,000.00 into ▉▉▉ bank account.

28. ▉▉▉ transferred $29,000.00 from ▉▉▉ and/or ▉▉▉'s bank account to ▉▉▉'s account at ▉▉▉.

29. After receiving the $29,000.00 from ▉▉▉, ▉▉▉ learned ▉▉▉ had made several expensive purchases.

30. Upon contacting the Florida lottery office, ▉▉▉ learned the ticket

redeemed was a $1,000,000.00 winning ticket.

31. ▉▉▉ demanded payment of all monies owed to him by ▉▉▉ but ▉▉▉ refused to pay ▉▉▉ any additional money.

This is where I stepped in to represent the Defendant. I am not sure how he found me, but I have represented hundreds, if not thousands, of people in the county where this occurred.

Typically, after a lawsuit is filed, both sides conduct discovery (interrogatories, admissions, request to produce, depositions, etc.). On behalf of my client, I did all of these.

The Plaintiff's attorney did nothing, and I mean nothing. He did not even take the Defendant's deposition. The *first* trial occurred in 2018.

On day one, we picked a jury, gave opening statements, and then the Plaintiff's lawyer called a couple of alleged witnesses to testify. I destroyed them! (Have I said "meth" was involved?)

The last witness for the day was the Plaintiff. The direct examination of the Plaintiff did not go well. He could barely remember his name, much less what happened over a year ago. (Direct exam is where your own lawyer asks you questions.)

Next was my cross-examination. It was brutal. I actually felt bad for the guy, but I had a job to do.

There was a brief recess before rebuttal. (During rebuttal, the Plaintiff's attorney tries to "clean up" the cross-examination testimony just elicited from the Plaintiff... in this case, by me). During rebuttal, it became abundantly clear the lawyer himself had been far too personally involved in this case. In fact, in one of my many objections and "sidebars" with the judge, the judge told the Plaintiff's lawyer he had interjected himself into the case in such a way that he could be called as a witness.

Although I agreed, I was stunned to hear the judge say that.

We adjourned for the day. I stayed up all night drafting an "Emergency Motion to Disqualify Plaintiff's Counsel." This was unprecedented stuff in the middle of trial, I can tell you that. The motion was filed at 7:23 a.m.

The next day, *shiz* really hit the fan! The hearing that morning was like something you see in a movie. But, after all was said and done, the judge granted a mistrial.

Remember, from a Defendant's perspective, "stall and delay" is typically the strategy. Although my client maintained he was the rightful owner of the ticket, you *never* know what a jury will do, never!

CHAPTER
ELEVEN

Well, almost two years went by before the Plaintiff's next attorney filed his "Notice of Appearance." Unfortunately for the Defendant, the new attorney was sharp. He knew what he was doing. He actually took the Defendant's deposition.

It did not go well. My client was very defensive. The two of them "got into it" several times during the deposition. I joined the fray, objecting to numerous lines of questioning. I even instructed my client not to answer many of the questions. That was a risky move, because if the judge thought the client should have answered the questions, I could've been sanctioned (i.e. fined a sum of money).

In 2022, the case went to trial again. The Plaintiff's team put on its case. The same people were called to the stand. (These witnesses were not too persuasive.) The Plaintiff was called to the stand. He looked worse now than he did in 2018. My cross-examination was pretty much the same as the last trial. The Plaintiff's final witness was the prior attorney who had been removed from the case.

Remember how the first trial ended? (Shiz hitting the fan!) Well, this is also how my cross-examination went. Though I knew what the prior attorney was saying was a load of crap, the jury was hearing it for the first time—they might have believed him, who knew. So, I went at him with both barrels. (I was pleasantly surprised that the judge—who had known the prior attorney since they worked together at the state attorney's office—let us go at it. It was kind of like the last two minutes in game seven of the Stanley Cup when the refs let 'em play.) First, I called the detective who investigated for the prior attorney. He testified he could not find any evidence supporting the Plaintiff's position. Next, I called the guy the Plaintiff claimed to have sold meth to in order to get the $20 he used to buy the lottery ticket. The witness denied this ever occurred.

During the Plaintiff's attorney's cross-examination of this witness, the Plaintiff, who looked strung out on meth, jumped out of his seat, took several steps towards the witness chair, and began screaming, "You're a liar! You're a liar!"

I thought the Plaintiff's attorney was going to have a stroke. The jury sat there frozen. The bailiff jumped up and escorted the

Plaintiff back to his seat. All the while, I was thinking, *This can't be good for them.* We took a brief recess so everyone could calm down.

The final witness was my client, the Defendant. He did as well as could be expected. He testified he initially gave the Plaintiff somewhere between two or three thousand dollars. He denied giving the Plaintiff $35,000. He did a good job of explaining the night the lottery ticket was won and the events leading up to it. Here was where the case went south: my client could not really explain why he gave the Plaintiff $29,000. His response when asked was simply, "That's what his lawyer asked for, so that's what I gave him," and "You will have to ask *them* why they asked for that amount." (Well, they had already explained to the jury why they asked for $29,000.) With that, we rested our case.

During closing arguments, the Plaintiff's attorney hammered home the sums of money the Defendant had given the Plaintiff after winning the lottery: initially $1,000, then $35,000, then the final payment of $29,000 (once confronted with the text messages). The attorney summarized that a million dollar lottery ticket "fell into the Defendant's hand" the morning of April 26, 2017, and the Defendant had taken advantage of his "meth head" friend.

You know when you're sitting there listening to someone talk and it either makes no sense, or it makes total sense? Let's just say... it didn't sound good from where I was sitting.

During my closing argument, I pointed out all the flaws in the Plaintiff's case. There was no direct evidence nor proof to substantiate the Plaintiff's claims. The detective had also found no evidence to substantiate the Plaintiff's claims, even after investigating the case for over a month. There was no evidence of the $35,000 payment. I talked about how the prior attorney manipulated the evidence, and how each witness for the Plaintiff either lied, or had a financial stake in the outcome of the case.

I did a great job, if I do say so myself. But—and don't you hate the word "but" sometimes?—I could not explain the text messages and the $29,000 wire transfer. I mean, I explained our position to the jury, but it was weak at best.

The jury was given the case around 2:30 p.m. This is the most difficult time for a trial attorney. Anyone who has tried as many cases as I have understands (and as I said before), you never know what a jury will do. So we sat: one hour, two hours, three hours, four hours, five hours...

Knock, knock.

"The jury has reached a verdict."

The jury returned to the court room. The foreperson handed the verdict to the bailiff, who then handed it to the judge. The judge looked at the verdict form, looked up at us, then turned to the jury and said, "Given your verdict for the Plaintiff, you are required to put a dollar figure in, if you intend on awarding him any money."

Are you kidding me?

So the jury returned to the deliberation room for another hour. Then they started sending out questions to the judge, which is allowed in Florida. None of the questions made any sense. The judge's answer to each question was simply this: "You have to rely on the evidence presented to you during the trial."

Needless to say, we lost. There was simply no way to explain the text messages and the $29,000 payment. Just that one little detail made a huge difference.

Don't Mess Around with the Reeds

Back around 2019, I got a stressed phone call from a friend of Ryan's and mine. This friend's marketing and branding company had been hired by a musician to design a logo for the musician's website. Now, this musician was also a lawyer, but he was a musician on the side, and the logo was for his music business. The musician paid up front, and signed the usual agreement (which included rounds of revisions to get the design to the client's liking, but no refunds for payment).

Our friend met with the musician several times—including being invited to the musician's home once, to see his musical instruments, discuss the logo design, and hear some of his music to get a feel for his brand as a musician. Then our friend designed the logo to the musician's specifications (including the use of a standard bass clef worked into the design), and sent it to the musician. He did not hear back for feedback, and no revisions were requested. After several months of attempting to contact the musician via email, phone calls, and texts, our friend delivered the final files, and closed out the project on his end.

Months later, the musician reached out and demanded a refund. He claimed that the logo our friend provided was not what he'd asked for, and that our friend owed him his money back. He also claimed that our friend's design was unoriginal, because he found similar designs online using the same symbol (the *bass clef* symbol, which is used in literally *all* types of imaging for music, and was also the symbol the musician himself had asked our friend to include in the design). Our friend reminded the musician of the no-refund policy, plus the attempts to contact him previously about revisions, and said he was unable to return the amount paid for the logo (which his business had since spent in expenses). Our friend is an entrepreneur and his company was a small business—at the time, it was a one-man operation, just him. He simply couldn't afford to return that money when he had, in fact, completed the design and delivered the product.

So the musician sued our friend for $750. What a joke! He even threatened to go after our friend's wife and their personal assets if our friend did not return that money. Our friend reached out to us in a panic... and Ryan and I stepped in to help.

This dragged on for months, despite our attempts to resolve it, and eventually it went to trial.

This musician was a real piece of work. You would've thought he was asking for millions of dollars. He literally sued our friend in small claims over $750, and represented himself.

Ryan and I represented our friend.

We had to take depositions. The musician-lawyer deposed our client for a couple of hours, then Ryan deposed the musician-lawyer for an hour or so... and the musician-lawyer had his partner sit in on the deposition.

(I got the feeling his partner was thinking, "What the heck are you doing? Why are you wasting time on this piddly crap?")

Things got rescheduled a few times, but finally, after several more months, we went to trial.

The judge who got our case that day didn't even usually take these types of cases. But she looked at the file, and how long our case had been on the docket, and she said, "You've been waiting a long time. Let's just proceed."

So we began... and it was clear that the musician-lawyer was outright lying. Even though our client had the text messages and the phone records, the musician-lawyer denied that our client had continued to try to contact him. Then he claimed that he had given our client feedback on the design in a quick phone call, but that our client had refused to make the requested changes. However, there was only one listing on the phone record showing he'd actually answered a call from our client, which totaled about forty-five seconds. And he directly lied about him and our client having ever met in person, saying our client had never been to his house.

Then the musician-lawyer called our client to the stand. Part of what our client said, again, was, "I went over to his house and he showed me this," etc.

And the musician-lawyer denied that had ever happened.

So I got up, and I asked our client, "Well, you've been to his house? Tell the judge what it looks like." So our client went into detail describing the fireplace, and what the musician-lawyer had here and there in his living room.

Then we called the musician-lawyer up again, and I said, "Mr. X, is that what your house looks like?"

"Well, yeah," he said, "but I don't know how he could know that."

"Well, he would know that if he had been there, wouldn't you agree?"

The guy was just an arrogant, lying jerk, and the judge wasn't buying what he was selling.

At one point, the musician-lawyer even told the judge, "Now, I don't know how much you know about music..."

Ryan was about to lodge an objection during the Plaintiff's case when I leaned over and said, "No, just wait. Look at the judge's face."

She was *not* happy about how the musician-lawyer talked down to her. So we just let the guy keep talking and dig his own hole.

In the end, it all came down to that phone call. Did this musician-lawyer, in fact, provide feedback to our client for revisions that our client ignored? And the judge said, "I just don't see how forty-five seconds could constitute any kind of meaningful feed-back for revisions on the design. I rule in favor of the Defendant."

And we won. Our client didn't owe the musician-lawyer a thing.

As we were walking out of the courtroom, I started singing the lyrics to "You Don't Mess Around with Jim" by Jim Croce.

Our client called us on the way home, and was like, "Yeah! *Yeah!* You guys were awesome!" He was all excited.

But the whole situation was ridiculous... This musician was just an absolute arrogant jerk to *everybody*, and we all knew he didn't have a case, but he just wouldn't let it go. He was a law-yer, and he thought he could bully our client and friend into giving back money that he wasn't rightfully owed.

The Reeds do not like bullies.

Letter to the School Board

This was a recent one... a situation where a school refused to allow a child's parents on campus, because of COVID restrictions, despite the student's clearly documented autism. Her parents had informed the school that they needed to escort their daughter to class, in order to prevent severe anxiety and a "meltdown." The school still refused. This was a violation of both the Americans with Disabilities Act and Florida's Parental Rights Act, and—quite frankly—just extremely unnecessary and inconsiderate on the part of the school.

I took on this case pro bono, and sent the following letter on behalf of my clients (image is on the next page):

December 23, 2021

████████ County Public Schools

████████

District ████████ County Schools

Principal ████████ School

RE: Our Client: ████████
        Student:

Dear Sir or Madam:

      Please be advised, Reed & Reed Law, PLLC, represents ████████ It appears the school may be in violation of the American Disabilities Act by failing to provide reasonable accommodations for ████, who is autistic and has ADHD. Further ████ Elementary appears to be in violation of Florida Parents' Bill of Rights Law by infringing on certain fundamental parental rights.

      The solution to the problem is simple, allow Mr. ████ to walk his daughter to the classroom door in the morning, he does not even have to enter the classroom and have an occasional lunch with his autistic daughter. Mr. ████ has no problem segregating from the rest of the students and staff at ████.

      I grew up in Brandon. I went to Yates Elementary (Principal Alice Hill), Horace Mann Jr High School (Principal Carlie Harris) and Brandon High School (Principal Orlan Bryant). None of these fine educators would have ever thought to prevent a parent from being involved in their students' education. Never!

      Finally, it is extremely disturbing that I had to get involved. All of you should be ashamed of yourselves!

                    Very truly yours,

                    REED & REED LAW, PLLC

                    PAUL S. REED
                    Attorney at Law

In the end, the school still didn't change anything. They brought the dad in and had a conversation, but that was it—which is a shame. But I'm still glad I wrote the letter. In my opinion, it's better to speak out about an injustice, when you see one, than to let it continue in silence just because you might not be able to change it.

If no one ever speaks up, the change will never come.

CHAPTER
ELEVEN

——————————————————— PAUL REED

Chapter 12

◆─○─────────────○─◆

Like Having a Lawyer
in the Family

Our tagline for Reed & Reed is, "It's like having a lawyer in the family." But for me, it's never been just a tagline.

I started Reed & Reed *with* my family. I became a lawyer *for* my family, to provide for them, and I returned to Brandon and stayed in Brandon to establish my practice because most of my family and friends *live* in Brandon.

This is my home. My team and my staff are all family and close friends, and many of my clients are my friends—whether they started that way or became friends later.

I've never been out to "get filthy rich" as a lawyer. I just wanted to provide for my family, make some kind of difference, and do good for my family, my friends, and my community.

To put something *good* into the world.

These days, money isn't a concern anymore. But injustices, mistakes, accidents that leave people injured with fear for how they'll cover their bills—those are still concerns. Those happen every day.

And that's why we keep on working, why we show up for our clients, why we continue to take on new ones, why we never turn off our phones.

I could tell you myself that being one of Reed & Reed's clients really is like having a lawyer in the family—but of course, I'm a lawyer, and they all say stuff like that, right? You probably wouldn't believe me. (Ha.)

You can, however, check our reviews online... or even my co-author's *Afterword*, which she'll include just after this chapter. Those reviews and statements say something about how we run our business, but more importantly, they say something about *how we feel about our clients.*

As soon as you walk in our door and sign your name on that line to work with us, *you're family.* We will be there for you—yes, even on our day off. Yes, even at 2 a.m.

The heart behind Reed & Reed today is the same as the heart I started with: I'm just a redneck from Brandon. I had no silver spoon.

You know what I did have? Family. Friends. People who were there for me. *That* is what people really need. Someone who will be there when they're hurt, or in trouble. Someone who actually cares.

It just makes it even more helpful if, occasionally, that someone is also a lawyer.

I hope this book has helped demonstrate that not *all* lawyers are just out to make money off their clients. Some of us are just good 'ol boys, grown from the sandy soil of orange groves and fed on burgers and Hershey bars, trying to do right by our families and our communities and trying to put some good back into the world.

It's the other side of the law, and it still happens, daily, right here in our office in Brandon.

God bless you... and if you live in the Brandon area and ever need a good personal injury lawyer, give Ryan or Jackie or me a call.

Our phones are always on.

—Paul

Afterword

————◆—◇——————————◇—◆————

A Note from Paul's Co-Author

(by Crystal Crawford)

I first met Paul Reed through my husband, Jason.

I knew of Reed & Reed—Paul's son, Ryan, was in Jason's business networking group, and my husband's company did Reed & Reed's social media marketing. I had even attended some parties and get-togethers the Reeds had hosted. I knew, from my husband's work as their social media marketer, and also from the billboards I'd seen around town, that Reed & Reed's motto was "Like having a lawyer in the family." I liked the motto—but lawyers have mottos, right? That doesn't necessarily mean they *live* by them.

When the kids and I were in a car accident in 2015, the first call my husband told me to make was to the Reeds. He gave me Ryan's cell phone number, and I called.

Their help was a Godsend. They helped me navigate everything from top to bottom, and made sure my kids and I all got the medical care we needed. They were kind, and compassionate, and took so much stress out of the process.

And then, a few months later, my husband and I were in another car accident. I didn't realize I was pregnant at the time of the crash, until I lost the baby.

Looking back, a lot about the months following that crash is a blur, but I remember Ryan saying to me, as we went to arbitration,

"I'm going to have to mention the miscarriage. You can step out of the room, if that makes things easier for you."

I stayed. I watched him fight for me. I watched him get us everything we needed for medical care, ongoing chiropractic care, and more. I watched him treat my loss with compassion, not like we were just another case—*like we were family.*

I didn't know Paul well, yet... not until he stepped in when one of my husband's design clients began harassing my husband and threatening our family, then sued my husband's company, claiming my husband had not delivered on their contract even though my husband had records and proof that he had. We did not have the money to hire a lawyer. At the time, we were barely getting by. Paul offered to take on the case *pro bono*. (Yes, my husband was *that* "hairball" case mentioned in this book.)

If you've never met Paul in person, he's a jovial guy. Friendly. But in the courtroom, my husband said Paul turned into a bulldog. He dismantled the other lawyer's case with straight logic and evidence, and got the entire suit dropped. He protected our family— by choice, because he wanted to help.

Since then, our kids have attended the Reeds' barbecues and a birthday party at Paul's house. We've attended holiday parties. My husband hops on a chat every single week with Paul for their *Live Feed Reeds* livestream, and he and Paul banter like friends. Because they are.

About a year ago (at the time of writing this), our only vehicle was stolen from in front of our house—on our daughter's eleventh birthday—by an overzealous towing company who then refused to give it back until we paid impound fees. I texted Paul. He answered my text with advice. When, a few minutes later, I realized the towing company had also damaged our tires, I called Paul.

He took my call with a friendly, "Hey, Troublemaker. What'd they do now?"

When I called again a while later because the towing company tried to make me sign some kind of waiver paperwork in order to release my vehicle, he answered that one, too.

He answered every single call. On a day off. While golfing with Ryan. In fact, I could hear Ryan in the background, chiming in, helping me, too.

"Ask them if they've heard of Reed & Reed," Paul told me. "Give them my cell number and tell them to call me." Paul was willing to fight for me, to make sure that company took care of the damages they'd caused. And when I apologized for bothering him, his reply was a cheerful, "You're not bothering me at all." It was—well, it was exactly like having a lawyer in the family.

In fact, earlier this year, Paul invited us over to spend the Fourth of July at his place. We grilled out, the kids swam in the pool, and we just hung out—Paul really does treat us like *family*.

That is who Paul Reed is. That is what he and his son Ryan, and Ryan's wife Jackie, have built their business around.

I haven't worked as closely with Jackie, but Jason has, and he says she's the same—they are all great lawyers, and they all genuinely care.

Later on the day our vehicle was taken, Paul told my husband, "Towing companies like this know that the average person can't afford to hire a lawyer. They bet on people just paying the $180 impound fee, instead. And the thing is, 99 percent of the time, they're right—which is why they get away with it. But *this* time... this is that 1 percent. This is *my* time."

(I still smile every time I think of that. It is just so... *Paul*.)

The more I've come to know Paul while working on this book, the more I see the core of who he is. Whatever preconceptions you may have had about lawyers, I can almost *guarantee* they won't apply to Paul—but if you've read this book, you already know that. Paul is down-to-earth and friendly and fun-loving, and if you hang around with him more than an hour or two, you'll probably end up part of some crazy adventure (or at least witnessing one). But when he's protecting the people of his community, there isn't anyone fiercer or more trustworthy to have at your side.

There's a reason Reed & Reed is one of the top legal firms in the Tampa Bay area, and it isn't just because of their skill (which they do have, in abundance). It's also because of their heart. Paul started with close to nothing—as you've read. He has lived in trailer parks and small suburban houses and one-bedroom urban apartments. He has scraped by, he has cried tears of gratitude when others gave their time and means to help him, and he has been that help for others. Paul now runs Reed & Reed in an office less than two miles from where he grew up, and he worked hard for every inch of the business he's built. Paul would be the first to tell you he isn't perfect. (There are probably some of his life stories that, by the time this goes to publication, were redacted from this book because the world just isn't ready!) But you'd be hard-pressed to find a better lawyer, or anyone with a bigger heart for the people of his community.

It is an honor to have been asked by Paul to help him write this book.

The first time Paul and I met to discuss this project, he ended the meeting by telling me, "By the time we've finished this, you and I will be like best friends—you'll probably know me better than anybody."

And let me just say, here in these pages is the chance for you to know Paul, too. This book shows "the other side of the law"—the struggle of how Paul got from there to here, the hardships and the triumphs and the insane, crazy stories you'd probably never believe if Paul didn't have photographic proof. But behind all that, and running through it, is the heart of a man who will take a random phone call on a day off and show up with a *"This is that 1 percent. This is my time"* when you need him.

Like family.

I hope you enjoyed his story, and that it helped remind you—like it does me—that there are good-hearted people out there, trying to put a little bit more good into the world every day.

Sincerely,

Crystal Crawford
(Co-author)

Paul's Famous Chili Recipe

Pretty much anyone who's been to a party at my house has had a chance to try my chili. It's become part of what I'm known for, so since I'm sharing my life story in this book, it just makes sense to share my secret chili recipe, too.

I hope you enjoy it!

Basic Ingredients

- 2 lbs of ground beef (93% lean beef is best)
- 1 16 oz hot sausage roll
- 3 large cans of diced tomatoes
- 1 cup of water
- 2 cans of pinto beans (do not drain)
- 2 cans of light red pinto beans (do not drain)
- 1 bag of frozen diced onions (if you want to dice a real onion, you can)
- 1 bag of frozen diced green peppers (if you want to dice a real green pepper, you can)
- 1 package of Wick Fowler's Texas Style 2 Alarm Chili Kit (Note: they no longer add salt so you MUST add it yourself... the amount is up to you.)

Now here is where you have to decide how spicy/hot you want the chili. It may take you several pots to figure out how you actually want it.

You can use one of the following:

- ½ a bottle of hot sauce
- 1 cup (or more) of diced jalapeno peppers (or cut up 5 or 6 fresh ones)
- 3 or 4 habanero peppers (Caution: wash your hands THOR-OUGHLY after handling these.)

Side note: the name of the recipe associated with the use of the habanero peppers is "#$% Flaming Chili!" (But with the actual word instead of the symbols used here, of course.)

Cooking Instructions:

1. You need at least a 12-quart pot.
2. Brown the meat (beef and sausage). Brown in a separate pan/skillet, or you can brown the meat in the large pot before adding the other ingredients, but drain the grease before adding the other ingredients.
3. Once the meat is brown, add that to the large pot (drain the grease).
4. Pour all of the other ingredients, including the 2 Alarm mix, into the large pot and stir thoroughly.
5. Cook for several hours on low to medium low, stirring often.

This recipe is great for football Sundays! I eat mine with sour cream, saltine crackers, and/or Fritos Scoops.

Acknowledgements

Not all my life stories or interesting cases are in this book. There could probably have been another chapter or two, but... we're taking some of those stories to the grave.

I would like to thank the Lord, first and foremost, for blessing me more than I could ever have imagined.

Thank you to my mom, for everything she's done, which is too much to list.

Thank you to my kids—Ryan, Brittany, and LeeAnn—you are who I live for. Thank you for putting up with me.

Thank you to my brothers: Keith, who's deceased and as you can see has been a large part of this book, and Jody, who helped make me and my life what it is.

To the Brandonites, both those listed in the book and those who aren't (but who may very well be in the next book): You know who you are. I would not be who I am or where I am without you.

To Crystal, for putting up with me with the patience of a saint: I literally could not have done this without you.

And lastly, to Jason, the Ed McMahon to my Johnny Carson: Thank you for designing the incredible book cover and making *Live Feed Reeds* what it is today.

Crystal and I would also like to thank our editor, Christy Freeman, for her help in shaping the early drafts of this book and catching all the places where we needed to explain more clearly; our early readers, Ryan Reed and Brittany Reed, for giving valuable feedback on the content of the book; our beta reader,

M.J. Padgett, for providing reader reactions and feedback on the story; and our proofreader, Erin Fielding, for ensuring our final product was polished and as error-free as possible.

And a big thank you to everyone else who has supported the creation of this book, too. We appreciate all of you.

About the Authors

For over 25 years, Paul Reed has argued cases in trial and appellate courts throughout Florida and the United States. He is a Florida Supreme Court Certified Circuit Court Mediator and is also licensed to practice in the United States Federal Court System. Paul brings extensive trial experience to the table after having represented clients in thousands of injury cases. He has achieved success for the victims of medical malpractice, automobile negligence, wrongful death, drowning cases, slip and falls, dog bites,  assault and battery, nursing home abuse, motorcycle crashes, defective products, bicycle accidents, and more.

Paul's legal efforts and creative advocacy have earned him a reputation for taking the most difficult cases to trial. His dedication to fighting negligence is reflected in his work and life. In 1999, Paul established the Mark Mahoney Memorial Scholarship Golf Tournament in order to honor his lifelong friend and teammate, Mark Mahoney, who passed away in an automobile accident. The golf tournament raises money for high school students who wish to attend Georgia Tech, Mark's alma mater.

Paul is an established trial lawyer and dedicated father of three children: daughters Brittany and LeeAnn; and son Ryan, who is now his partner. Paul is now practicing law out of an office located in Brandon, Florida off of Parsons Ave. You can find him online at http://needreed.com.

Crystal Crawford is an indie author, wife, homeschool mom, freelance editor, and writing instructor, and has also served for several years as the Director of a nonprofit class program for homeschooling families. While from Temple Terrace, Florida, she now lives in Brandon, a few miles from the Reed & Reed office. In addition to nonfiction projects like this book, Crystal writes young adult fantasy (and a smattering of other genres) and co-runs *PirateCat Publishing*, an online reading platform and interactive community for clean young adult fiction (available at http://piratecatpublishing.com). Crystal  lives with her husband, their four kids, and her one-eyed cat, who have all supported her dream of writing and drinking far too much coffee. You can find out more about her books, ongoing serials, and other published works at https://ccrawfordwriting.com.

www.ingramcontent.com/pod-product-compliance
Lightning Source LLC
Chambersburg PA
CBHW050446150626
46551CB00029B/1799